Boeing 737

Written by Robert W. Tidwell

At The Gate®

Cover Art by Don Greer

Line Illustrations by Melinda Turnage

Squadron Signal® Publications

(Front Cover) NASA used the prototype 737 for a battery of experiments, one of the most important of which was the Wind Shear Sensor Flight Test. These experiments led to means by which wind shear could be detected so as to allow pilots time to react and possibly save lives.

(Back Cover) In mid-2009, Continental Airlines painted one of its new 737-900ERs in the company's classic 1950s "Blue Skyways" livery to celebrate 75 years of service. In late 2010, Continental airlines announced a merger with the United Airlines. The new airline's livery will consist of the existing Continental livery with a simple "United" title replacing the Continental title.

About the At The Gate Series®

This series is similar to the Walk Around series that focuses on military aircraft. Books in this genre concentrate on commercial or private aircraft that have been used or are currently operated by carriers worldwide in a variety of interesting and colorful liveries.

 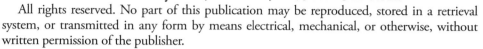
Military/Combat Photographs and Snapshots

If you have any photos of aircraft, armor, soldiers, or ships of any nation, particularly wartime snapshots, please share them with us and help make Squadron/Signal's books all the more interesting and complete in the future. Any photograph sent to us will be copied and returned. Electronic images are preferred. The donor will be fully credited for any photos used. Please send them to:

Squadron/Signal Publications
1115 Crowley Drive
Carrollton, TX 75006-1312 U.S.A.
www.SquadronSignalPublications.com

(Title Page) Alaska Airlines also celebrated its 75th anniversary and selected a 737-890 to wear the livery used in the 1940s. The aircraft also features a large "75" on the vertical stabilizer. (Alaska Airlines)

Acknowledgments

This book would not have been possible without the help and support of Air Canada, Alaska Airlines, Continental Airlines, Deutsche Lufthansa, Southwest Airlines, Sunil Gupta, Kulula Airlines, Zip Airlines, Axel Juengerich, Bob Garrard, Bill Shemley, Rick Schlamp, Denis Desmond, KLM Airlines, Erik Johannesson, Mikael Persson, Trevor Hall, Savvas Garozis, Christian Herbert Schöpf, Bob Bogash, Christopher Iwane, and Phillip Capper.

Dedication

To my friends and family and to all who build, fly, and maintain these wonderful machines.

Introduction

The Boeing 737 in its various versions and guises is a common sight at airports around the world. This ubiquitous aircraft serves short- and medium-range routes and is on its way to entering long-range service. As of the time of writing, more than 6,000 aircraft in this family have been built and more than 4,000 remain in service in 190 countries and territories. This one series accounts for just over 33 percent of Boeing's orders for commercial aircraft.

The 737 story begins on 11 May 1964 with the start of a design study for an aircraft intended to supplement the 727. In charge of the work were two of Boeing's most accomplished engineers: Joseph F. "Joe" Sutter (who is better known for another Boeing icon – the 747), and John E. "Jack" Steiner, the father of the 727. Their task was to develop an 85-seat jetliner with a range of about 575 miles that could compete with the Douglas DC-9 and the British Aircraft Corporaton's BAC One-Eleven, both of which were inspired by the Sud Aviation Caravelle. At that time there were several mid-range jetliners on the market, but Steiner believed that Boeing, at the end of the day, could simply "build a better mousetrap."

The two men settled on a twin-engine design and also decided to simplify matters by borrowing elements from the 707 and the 727. The 707 was the basis for the fuselage cross section, and the engines, Pratt & Whitney JT8D series low-bypass turbofans, were also used on the 727. Steiner and Sutter knew that Douglas had decided on tail-engined designs for its DC-9 and initially considered a similar arrangement for the 737. They were concerned, however, that such tail-engine designs were prone to deep stalls.

Sutter refined the overall 737 design by trying different engine placements on a three-view aircraft drawing that omitted the engines. Ultimately, Sutter and Steiner resolved to put the engines under the wing. This design was particularly appropriate, since the 707-derived fuselage was wider than that of the DC-9 and a rear-engine arrangement would have generated negative aerodynamic effects. Inspired by the outer engine mounting for the Boeing B-47 Stratojet, Sutter decided to ensure good ground clearance by dispensing with pylons and mating the engines directly to the underside of the wing.

The next major consideration was the design of the wing itself. The design team emphasized that it should have excellent take-off and landing performance. The wing itself had a modest sweep to balance high and low speed performance and the main spars had a dihedral of 6° with a bit more cant outboard of the engine mounts. The 737 was the first Boeing aircraft to have both spars cranked and the decision continues to benefit the aircraft to this day; this design feature provided the aircraft with excellent fuel capacity relative to the wing's span.

Weight reduction was another benefit of the underslung engine configuration. The first structural integrity tests on the wing prompted a slight redesign and some strengthening. Overall, the final airframe was 1,550 pounds lighter than tail-engined designs of comparable size. The wing-mounted engine design also increased the amount of space in the airframe available for passenger seating and buffered some of the engine noise. Placement of the engines on the wings also facilitated maintenance at ground level.

When the prototype design was complete, the length and wingspan were nearly identical, prompting some to call the 737 the "square jet."

The first airline to buy the 737 was Lufthansa, which ordered 22 aircraft in February 1965, but asked Boeing to "stretch" the original design of the airframe to enable it to accommodate 100 passengers. The next version, the -200, responded to United Airlines' request for additional seating capacity by "stretching" the fuselage to accommodate 120 seats. By the time Boeing delivered the first of the -100s in December 1967, 19 airlines in 10 countries had placed orders for 185 of the 737s.

The good start notwithstanding, Boeing's 737 program nearly died in its infancy. The 737 had to struggle for engineering and financial resources because of the company's heavy investment in the 747. By 1970, Boeing was seriously considering raising capital by selling the whole 737 program to the Japanese aerospace industry. Transporting the production line to Japan was feasible, since Boeing had built portable production jigs for the 737 to facilitate moving the production line to Wichita, Kansas.

Boeing gave serious thought to closing the production line when orders for the 737 plummeted during the oil crisis of the early 1970s. Within a few years, however, the crisis passed, Boeing introduced the 737-200 Advanced, and orders for 737s rebounded. The 737-200 Advanced was the culmination of a handful of refinements in the -200 that improved the range and payload of the aircraft; these alterations became the production standard for the -200 from aircraft No. 135 onward. In the later 1970s, advances in avionics and engine technology helped spur further developments in 100-to-150 seat short-to-medium range airliner market. In 1981, Boeing launched the 737-300 powered by CFM International CFM56 series high-bypass turbofan engines and had ready orders from Southwest Airlines and USAir. This version served as the foundation for two further generations of 737s – the Classic and Next Generation. The "classic" 737s consist of the -300 through the -500. The Next Generation aircraft consist of the -600 through -900, and in 2011, Boeing announced further upgrades to the 737. The -700, -800, and -900 will feature refinements in the engine nacelles and other undisclosed changes that promise to increase fuel efficiency and lower operations costs. The 737 story continues.

Alone in the hangar stands the first of the breed that would produce thousands of stable mates. Engineers, designers, and craftsmen tended to the aircraft around the clock as she was assembled. The prototype was rarely alone in the hangar as personnel made sure that everything in the aircraft went together perfectly. (Bob Bogash)

Boeing 737-100

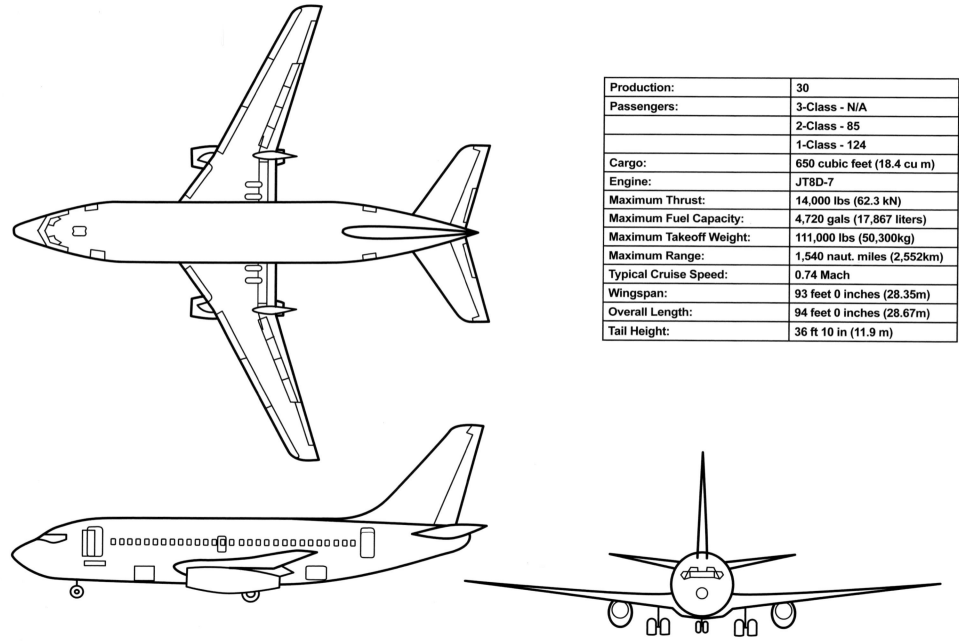

Production:	30
Passengers:	3-Class - N/A
	2-Class - 85
	1-Class - 124
Cargo:	650 cubic feet (18.4 cu m)
Engine:	JT8D-7
Maximum Thrust:	14,000 lbs (62.3 kN)
Maximum Fuel Capacity:	4,720 gals (17,867 liters)
Maximum Takeoff Weight:	111,000 lbs (50,300kg)
Maximum Range:	1,540 naut. miles (2,552km)
Typical Cruise Speed:	0.74 Mach
Wingspan:	93 feet 0 inches (28.35m)
Overall Length:	94 feet 0 inches (28.67m)
Tail Height:	36 ft 10 in (11.9 m)

737-100

Production of the first series of 737s started on 4 November 1964 and the aircraft first took to the air on 9 April 1967 with pilot Brien Wygle and copilot Lew Wallick at the controls. The first eight airframes rolled off the assembly line in Plant II, where B-17s were built during WWII. The Pratt & Whitney JT8D-1 was the original powerplant chosen during the design phase of the 737-100, but Boeing had opted to switch to the JT8D-7 by the time that negotiations with Lufthansa were concluded. The -7 was rated to generate the same thrust as the -1, but at higher ambient temperatures. With its improved performance, the JT8D-7 became the standard powerplant for the -100 series. The fuselage consisted of an aluminum alloy semi-monocoque structure with forged alloy main frames and rolled alloy intermediate frames. The wing was a cantilever design with twin aluminum alloy spars. In aircraft made after 1984, the ailerons were constructed of graphite composite material.

Avionics were often tailored to the operator, but the standard equipment satisfied FAA Category II low-weather minimum standards. When fitted out with optional equipment, however, the aircraft met Category IIIA criteria.

Only 30 737-100s were built. Lufthansa bought 22, five were sold to Malaysia Airlines, and two went to the Colombian airline, Avianca. The last airworthy -100, which first flew on 12 June 1967, was retired from Aero Continente of Peru in 2005.

This Continental Airlines 737-130 had previously been in the service of People Express, hence the PE at the end of the FAA registration. Only 30 of the 737-100s were produced, so these aircraft changed hands many times during their service lives. (Joe Meneely)

Bill Allen, the president of Boeing from 1945 to 1968, greets assembled employees and members of the press on the 737's christening day. Allen guided the company from near stagnant production just after WWII to the transition into the jet age. (Bob Bogash)

Much of the cockpit of a 737-100 would be familiar pilot of the 1940s and 1950s. This -100 spent many years with Faucett Peru, one of Peru's oldest airlines. (Victor A. Potesta)

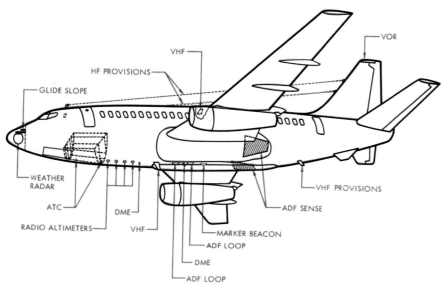

The 737, like other modern commercial aircraft, is packed with an array of radio equipment used for navigation, communication, and flight instrumentation. The antennas in the early -100 and -200 series were almost identical, but the -200s did not have HF cable antennas running from the fuselage to the vertical stabilizer; instead, the HF antenna was located inside the leading edge of the vertical stabilizer.

Many of Boeing's management occupy seats on a platform next to the first 737 during the ceremony marking the aircraft's christening on 17 January 1967. The event was an occasion for speeches on the importance of the aircraft to the company and what was expected of it in the future. Seen in the background is Lufthansa's first 737. (Bob Bogash)

The designers of the 737 worked to pack as many seats as possible into what was originally a compact twin-jet airliner. Airlines seeking to introduce jet service to short and medium-haul routes were impressed by the fact that most of the available volume on the 737 was devoted to seating and baggage.

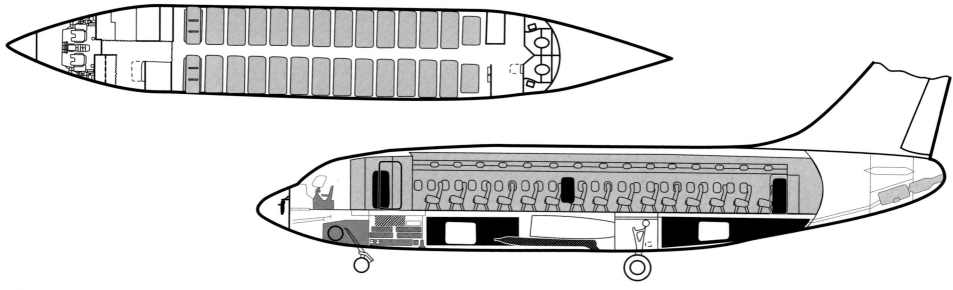

Boeing 737-200

Production:	1,114
Passengers:	3-Class – N/A
	2-Class – 97 (102 737-200Adv.)
	1-Class - 136
Cargo:	875 cu ft (24.78 cu m)
Engine:	JT8D-9A
	JT8D-15A
	JT8D-17
	JT8D-17R
Maximum Thrust:	14,500 lbs (64.5 kN)
	15,500 lbs (68.9 kN)
	16,000 lbs (71.2 kN)
	17,400 lbs (77.4 kN)
Maximum Fuel Capacity:	4,780 gals (18,094 liters)
	5,160 gals (19,533 liters) -200Adv
Maximum Takeoff Weight:	115,500 (52,400kg)
	128,100 (58,100kg) -200Adv
Maximum Range:	2,300 nm (4,260km)
Typical Cruise Speed:	0.74 Mach
Wingspan	93 ft 0 in (28.35m)
Overall Length:	100 ft 2 in (30.53m)
Tail Height:	36 ft 10 in (11.9m)

737-200

Almost as soon as production of the -100 began, Boeing realized that most airlines wanted a slightly greater passenger load. To extend the fuselage, Boeing engineers added a 36-inch section forward of the wing and a 40-inch section aft of the wing. The addition allowed the aircraft to carry a maximum of 136 passengers. All the rest of the aircraft's dimensions remained unchanged, although the increased passenger load necessitated a more powerful engine. Boeing chose the latest version of the JT8D engine, the JT8D-9, which was rated at 14,500 pounds.

The new 737 series was launched on 5 April 1965 with an order from United Airlines for 40 aircraft. The first -200 took to the air on 8 August 1967, but flight tests revealed that the -200 experienced 5 percent more drag than expected. Boeing engineers conducted wind tunnel and flight tests for a year and made a number of aerodynamic modifications. In March 1969, the redesigned flaps and thrust reversers became standard from aircraft 135 onward and free retrofit kits were offered for active aircraft.

The -200 featured updated avionics and automatic flight control system. In addition there are four commercial subtypes of the -200: the -200 Advanced, -200C, -200QC, and the -200 High Gross Weight Structure. The -200 featured improved fuel efficiency, aerodynamic improvements, more powerful engines, and automatic wheel brakes. The -200C is a convertible passenger/cargo version of the -200 Advanced. The aircraft features a large cargo door and a roller system in the floor. The -200QC is similar to the -200C, but can be quickly converted to passenger use. The High Gross Weight version was designed for long-distance operations.

A Lufthansa 737-230 Advanced (c/n23153) wears the company's striking two-color and natural metal color scheme that was worn well into the late 1980s. Lufthansa was a launch partner for the -100 and was one of the largest customers for the -200. The -200 was one of the most prolific of the 737 family with 1,114 manufactured. (Deutsche Lufthansa)

The right side cargo doors are open and ready for baggage transfer. Like many commercial aircraft, 737s often serve with several airlines over their lifetimes. This 737-2H4, registry N7381F, is in the Continental livery that it wore from 1986 to 1993. Prior to service with Continental, this ship served Frontier Airlines, Southwest Airlines, and PSA. (Phillip Capper)

In 2000, Air Canada acquired Canadian, and this aircraft, a Canadian 737-217 Advanced, registry C-GCPX (cn 22341), wears the transitional livery that combines the Air Canada livery on the vertical stabilizer with the short-lived "proud wings" livery that Canadian introduced in 1999. (Brian Losito / Air Canada)

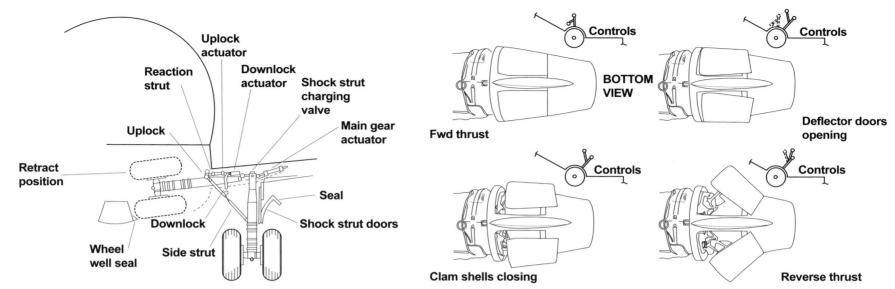

Fwd thrust

BOTTOM VIEW

Deflector doors opening

Clam shells closing

Reverse thrust

One feature of the 737 that remained the same from the -100 on to the -900ER was the general design of the main landing gear. In order to save weight, the main gear wells were designed without covers for the main gear wheels. To compensate for the lack of wheel well doors, the wheel covers for the outside wheels are aerodynamic and an inflatable seal is located around the edge of the wheel well opening.

The 737-100 and 737-200 used Pratt & Whitney JT8D series low-bypass turbofan engines. The thrust reversers on the aircraft consisted of a hydraulically-operated pair of deflectorl doors that formed part of the afterbody of the engine nacelle. An inner set of doors redirects the thrust to the clamshell doors which deflect the exhaust gasses forward.

The 737-200 was little different from the -200. The overall arrangement of the two versions was the same, but the -200 had a pair of plugs at stations 520 and 727. The plugs were 36 inches and 40 inches respectively. This allowed the -200 to carry a maximum of 130 passengers with a 28 inch seat pitch.

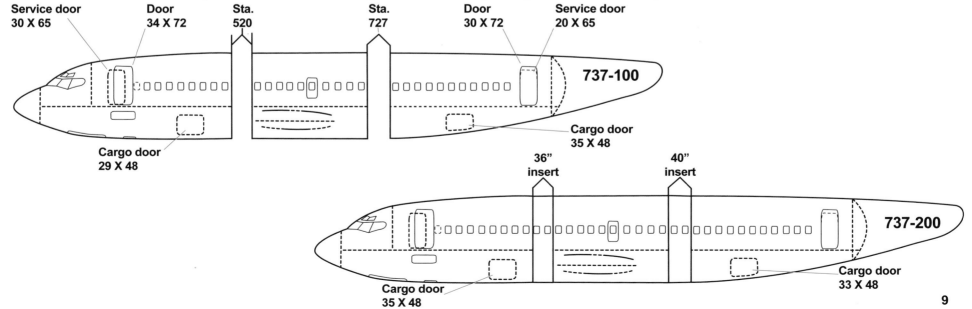

Service door 30 X 65

Door 34 X 72

Sta. 520

Sta. 727

Door 30 X 72

Service door 20 X 65

737-100

Cargo door 29 X 48

Cargo door 35 X 48

36" insert

40" insert

737-200

Cargo door 35 X 48

Cargo door 33 X 48

The flexible 737-200 Combi carries passengers and cargo at the same time. The large cargo door of this Canadian North 737-275C is open and ready to accept Unit Load Devices (ULDs or "pods") in the forward half of the main deck. Passengers are seated aft of the cargo pods. (Brian Pressey)

With its flight spoilers and ground spoilers fully extended, a Delta Express 737-232A undergoes an overhaul. Its flaps are extended and some of the flap track fairings have been removed. The wing root fairings have been removed exposing the wing root and some of the otherwise covered fuselage. (Gregg Stansbery)

The 737-200s were built in greater quantities and served longer than the preceding -100s. This -200 cockpit features only a couple of digital-age elements on the forward electronic control panel. (Luke Cranitch)

Aviacsa was a Mexican airline that served domestic routes and made international flights to Las Vegas, Nevada. This 737-201 is one of the 24 737-200s that served in its fleet. The airline, which ceased operations in 2010 after a series of financial troubles, has been reorganized and is currently operating under the direction of Grupo Madero. (Denis Desmond)

Until 2006, Delta Airlines operated 61 -200s like this 737-232 seen at Hartsfield-Jackson Atlanta International Airport, one of the airline's largest hubs. Delta was among the last major carriers to fly the -200s. (Jeffrey W. Williams)

This 737-242 (registry C-GNDM) was delivered to Quebec-based Nordair, an airline later sold to Calgary-based Pacific Western Airlines in 1987. Shortly thereafter, Pacific Western became part of Air Canada. (Air Canada)

This 737-228 Advanced was ordered by Air France in 1983. The aircraft later went on to Sicilia Airlines; then to Nationwide Airlines, a low-cost carrier in South Africa; and finally flew with Shaheen Air of Pakistan in 2010. (John Meneely)

This 737-230C is one of three 737 freighters operated by the airfreight company German Cargo, a wholly-owned subsidiary of Lufthansa. The 737 cargo version is easily spotted by its small number of windows around the cabin. (Mikael Persson)

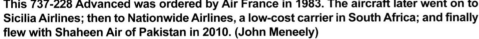

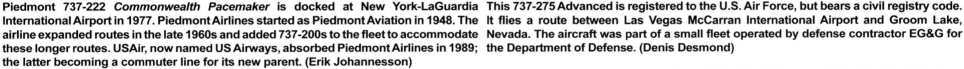

Piedmont 737-222 *Commonwealth Pacemaker* is docked at New York-LaGuardia International Airport in 1977. Piedmont Airlines started as Piedmont Aviation in 1948. The airline expanded routes in the late 1960s and added 737-200s to the fleet to accommodate these longer routes. USAir, now named US Airways, absorbed Piedmont Airlines in 1989; the latter becoming a commuter line for its new parent. (Erik Johannesson)

This 737-275 Advanced became part of the Canadian Airlines fleet after that airline purchased Pacific Western in 1987. Air Canada and Canadian Airlines, in turn, merged in 2001. The aircraft is seen here wearing the Air Canada livery in use from 1994-2004. (Air Canada)

This 737-275 Advanced is registered to the U.S. Air Force, but bears a civil registry code. It flies a route between Las Vegas McCarran International Airport and Groom Lake, Nevada. The aircraft was part of a small fleet operated by defense contractor EG&G for the Department of Defense. (Denis Desmond)

The Canadian airline Transair purchased this 737-2A9C, named *Fort York,* in 1970 when the airline expanded its international routes. Transair used the 737-200s mostly for charter flights to Florida, the Caribbean, and Mexico. Pacific Western Airlines purchased Transair in 1979. The acquisition of Transair was made easier by virtue of the two airlines operating some of the same aircraft. (Air Canada)

This 737-204C still features a high-frequency radio aerial cable running from the vertical stabilizer to a connection on the top of the fuselage. Eventually, many airlines replaced the HF cable aerials with HF aerials located inside the leading edge of the vertical stabilizer. (Erik Johannesson)

The 737-100 and -200 were equipped with JT8D-series low-bypass turbofan engines. The -100s' JT8D-7s generated 14,000 pounds of thrust. The -200s were fitted with four different JT8D engines. The earlier -200s featured JT8D-9As rated at 14,500 pounds thrust each, while later models used the JT8D-17Rs rated at 17,400 pounds. (Chris Brady)

When viewed head-on, one can see what made the 737 competitive in its class: width comparable to a long-range airliner. This feature was a plus for airlines seeking to maximize earnings on short- and medium-range routes. (Canadian Airlines)

From this angle, the close relationship between the fuselage of the 707 and the 737 is apparent. Both aircraft share the same fuselage cross section that enabled the 737 to offer six-abreast seating in a short- to medium-range airliner. (Trevor Hall)

This 737-204 wears the Britannia Airways livery used through the 1980s. In the late 1960s, the airline decided to offer jet service and chose the 737 instead of aircraft from BAC, despite pressure from the British Government. In response to this decision, the government levied a 14 percent tax on the American-made aircraft. (Trevor Hall)

Sometimes bankrupt airlines do not disappear completely from the world. After Braniff International Airlines declared bankruptcy in 1982, a new airline, Braniff Inc., was formed from the assets, such as this 737-222 belonging to the bankrupt carrier, and focused on domestic routes. Braniff, Inc. shuttered in 1990. (Trevor Hall)

Hispania Airlines was founded in 1982 with the purpose of providing charter flights from Britain, Germany, and France to resorts in Spain. The airline started service with two SE 210 Caravelles, but later replaced them with three 737-200s like this 737-248C. (Trevor Hall)

Luxair, the flag carrier for Luxembourg, was founded in 1961 with the purpose of connecting the small European nation with major cities in Europe. The airline started with Fokker F27 truboprops and expanded operations with the purchase of its first 737s such as this 737-229. This aircraft bears the airline's early livery. (Trevor Hall)

This view of a CanJet 737-296 on approach displays the aircraft's distinctive triple-slotted flaps. The flaps, spoilers, and flight controls were powered by two hydraulic systems: System A was powered by two engine-driven pumps, while System B, a backup, was powered by electrically-driven pumps. (Axel Juengerich)

This Hapag-Lloyd 737-2K5 Advanced on final approach provides a good illustration of the short-field abilities of the 737. The 737's wing features triple-slotted flaps, leading edge flaps outboard of the engines, and Krueger flaps inboard of the engines. Not visible in this photograph are the ground spoilers and flight spoilers. (Axel Juengerich)

This Lacsa 737-230 Advanced exhibits a normal approach attitude for a 737. The 737-200s feature hydraulically-actuated flight controls with a mechanical backup. The rudder has its own separate hydraulically-powered system and servo. (Axel Juengerich)

The 737-200 Advanced, like this example, serving with Vanguard Airlines, was designed with short field performance in mind. The goal of the -200 Advanced was to offer a twin-jet airliner that could operate from the shorter airfields often found in countries outside Europe and North America. (Axel Juengerich)

One of the constant features of the 737 is the presence of Krueger flaps inboard of the engines. These flaps are deployed during takeoff and landing to increase the camber of the wing and enhance lift at low speeds. Unlike a leading edge slat, a Krueger flap is hinged at the front and deploys from under the leading edge of the wing. (Chris Brady)

Star Peru previously operated eight 737-200s in its fleet. The aircraft fit well into the airline's almost exclusively domestic route structure. (Savvas Garozis)

The -200 has practically become an icon of the 737 family, because of the high production numbers for the type. With over 1,000 airframes built and good short-field performance, the -200 has seen service in nearly every nation. Even though most major airlines have retired their -200s in favor of -500s or similar aircraft, many charter and private operators continue to fly the type. (Phillip Capper)

Canadian Pacific Air Lines, also known for a time as CP Air, started as a small bush operation and grew to become a large airline with national and international routes. The airline used 737-200s, like this 737-217, for its routes in Canada and routes to the United States. (Bob Garrard)

The 737-200QC can serve as either a freight or passenger aircraft. To hasten the change, sidewalls and overhead bins remain intact, and pallets with pre-attached seats are loaded through the portside cargo door. (Phillip Capper)

The 737's short-field performance allowed the aircraft to be used by airlines in countries where aircraft had to land and take off from semi-prepared runways made of packed gravel. Some operators opted to have a "gravel kit" fitted to their 737-200s so that they could operate from such airfields with little threat of damage. This privately-owned -200 is fitted with a gravel kit. (Bob Garrard)

The deflector plate is very noticeable on aircraft equipped with a gravel kit. The plate is attached to the nose gear and has slits for the nose wheels. The deflector plate is sturdy and prevents damage to the underside of the aircraft from gavel and stones that can be kicked-up when the nose wheel is rolling at landing or takeoff speed. (Ted Brown)

Aircraft equipped with a gravel kit feature a modified nose gear well. The fairing on the forward end of the well allows the nose gear to retract and forces the deflector plate to change position and form part of the nose gear well doors. (Ted Brown)

The spring loaded hinges ensure that the plate remains parallel to the ground when the nose gear is extended. The plate is designed to be rugged and light weight. (Ted Brown)

The gravel kit also includes a diffuser attached to the underside of each intake lip. These deceptively simple tubes use some of the bleed air from the engines to disrupt the airflow immediately below and in front of the engine and prevent ingestion of loose gravel. (Ted Brown)

This United Airlines 737-222 was the first 0f 1,114 -200s delivered. The airline received 74 737-200s and was one of the largest operators of the type. United Airlines flew -200s until 2011. The -200s also wore several different versions of the United Airlines livery over the years. In 1973, the airline commissioned the famous graphic designer Saul Bass to create a new logo for the airline and the result was the "tulip" design that is seen on this aircraft. Saul Bass also designed Continental Airlines' "jet stream" logo which was used until the early 1990s. After the merger of Continental and United, the new livery is a hybrid of their recent liveries. This aircraft displays the version of the livery used from 1974 until 1993. (Axel Juengerich)

Boeing 737-300

Production:	1,113
Passengers:	3-Class - N/A
	2-Class - 128
	1-Class - 149
Cargo:	1,068 cubic feet (30.2 cu m)
Engine:	CFM56-3B-1
	CFM56-3B-2
Maximum Thrust:	20,000 lbs (89 kN)
	22,000 lbs (97.9 kN)
Maximum Fuel Capacity:	6,311 gals (23,890 liters)
Maximum Takeoff Weight:	140,000 lbs (63,500kg)
Maximum Range:	2,270 naut. miles (4,204km)
Typical Cruise Speed:	0.74 Mach
Wingspan (without winglets)	94 feet 9 inches (28.9m)
Wingspan (with winglets)	102 feet 1 inch (31.1m)
Overall Length:	109 feet 7 inches (33.4m)
Tail Height:	36 feet 6 inches (11.1m)

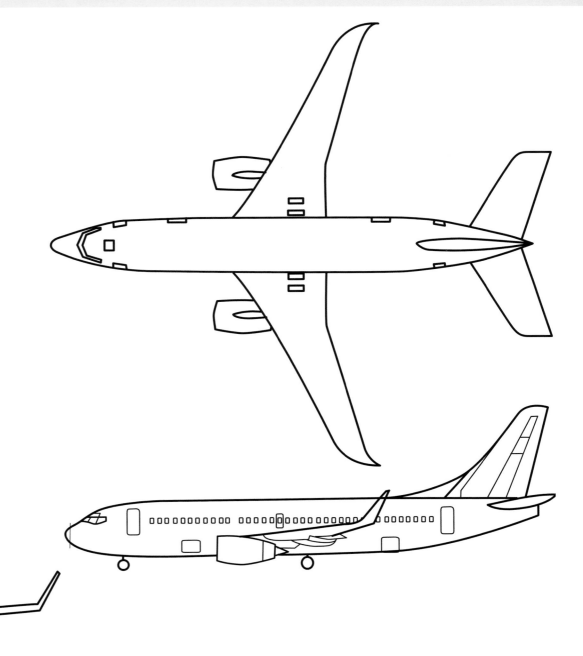

737-300

In March 1981, Boeing announced that it would introduce a new version of the 737. The -300 was originally conceived as little more than a simple stretch of the -200, but Boeing decided to drop the JT8D series of engine from the design in favor of the more fuel-efficient CFM56 high-bypass turbofans. Another reason for switching to the CFM56 was the necessity to comply with the proposed International Civil Aviation Organization (ICAO) Stage 3 noise limits. What made the new version attractive to customers of the -200 was that the -300 shared an 80% airframe parts commonality with its predecessor and could use the same ground handling equipment as the -200. The aerodynamic improvements of the -300 included an altered profile for the vertical stabilizer and modified leading edge slats.

Other improvements in the -300 were internal. The -300 benefitted from advances made during the 757's development, including improved overhead stowage bins and improved cabin lighting. Another technology transfer from the 757 was the introduction of electronic flight instruments, which were available to 737-300 customers on request.

In April 2011, a five-foot long breach formed in the roof of a Southwest Airlines aircraft, which had to divert to a military airbase in Arizona; however, there were no serious injuries. National Transportation Safety Board inspectors found cracks in lap joints adjacent to the hole. Inspections revealed that three other Southwest Airlines aircraft were developing cracks in lap joints in the same area of the fuselage and Boeing issued a maintenance bulletin for -300 operators with aircraft that had comparable flight-cycle times (approximately 39,000 flight cycles).

The baggage holds on the 737 are spacious for the aircraft's class and the 737-300 has a total baggage capacity of 1,068 cubic feet divided between two baggage holds. The forward baggage hold has a volume of 425 cubic feet and the aft hold has a capacity of 643 cubic feet. (James Covington)

In the late 1970s Boeing engineers looked for ways to improve the efficiency and performance of the 737. The result was the 737-300 which possessed a lengthened fuselage, new engines, and aerodynamic refinements. The earliest interest in the -300 came from USAir (now, US Airways) and Southwest Airlines which placed the first orders in 1981. (Denis Desmond)

British Airways operated 737-300s like this 737-382 from 1988 to 2009. The airline continues to fly 737-400s in its fleet of 237 aircraft. British Airways 737s operate from London Gatwick Airport. (Christian Herbert Schöpf)

America West was founded in 1981 in Tempe, Arizona, and commenced operations in 1983 with three leased 737s. The airline expanded quickly and purchased 11 737s like this 737-33A to serve it expanding routes. America West merged with US Airways in 2005. (Denis Desmond)

The basic design of the main landing gear has remained the same and has only been improved over the years to accommodate the demands of the various models of this long-serving aircraft. Each strut accommodates two wheels and the outside wheel features an aerodynamic cover, since the 737 design lacks a wheel well door. (Robert W. Tidwell)

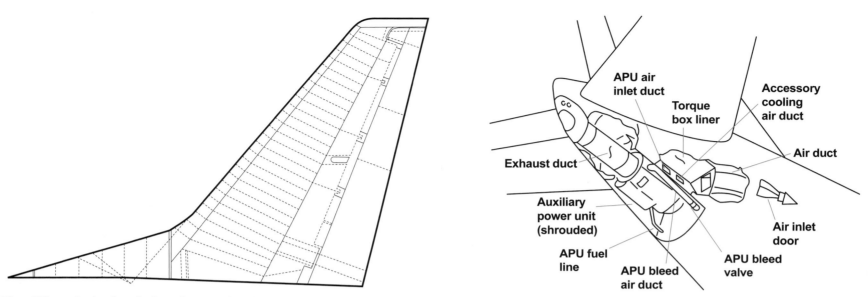

APU air
inlet duct

Torque
box liner

Accessory
cooling
air duct

Air duct

Exhaust duct

Air inlet
door

Auxiliary
power unit
(shrouded)

APU bleed
valve

APU fuel
line

APU bleed
air duct

The -300 marked a few design changes that became standard on following 737s. One change was to the leading edge of the vertical stabilizer. Previously curved, its new, more angular design (seen here) improved airflow around the stabilizer.

The general arrangement of the Auxiliary Power Unit (APU) remained the same throughout the 737 family. The same general APU arrangement and placement can be found on 737s from the -100 on through the -900ER

The 737-300 marked a new chapter in the 737's story. With the -300, Boeing abandoned the JT8D low-bypass turbofans in favor of the more powerful and efficient CFM56 family of high-bypass turbofan engines. CFM56 engines of various types have powered 737s since the introduction of the -300. The new engines required a redesigned engine mounting system.

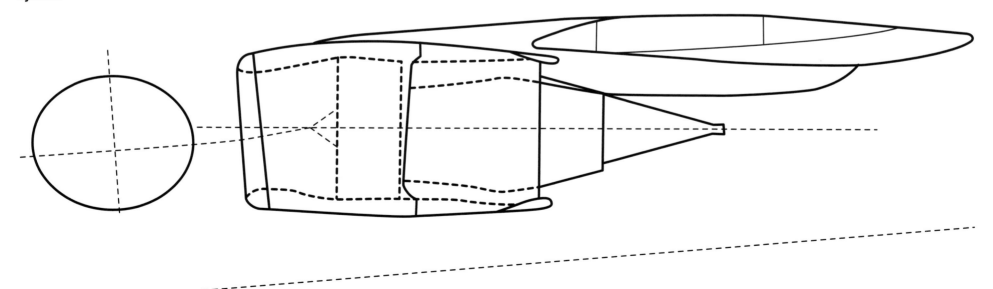

Western Pacific Airlines started service in 1995 with eight 737-300 aircraft including this 737-3B7 which Delta Airlines purchased in the wake of Western Pacific's bankruptcy. When this aircraft operated with Western Pacific, it featured an advertisement for Colorado Tech University painted on the fuselage. (Denis Desmond)

Skywings International is a Macedonian airline that started service in 2009. The airline started with this lone 737-33A leased from Hamburg International. (Christian Herbert Schöpf)

Transaero is a Russian airline that was founded in 1990. The majority of the airline's fleet is Boeing aircraft including this 737-329 which is one of only two 737-300s in the fleet. (Christian Herbert Schöpf)

Copenhagen-based Jettime started operations in 2006. The company operates a charter and wet-lease service with seven 737s. This 737-3Y0 is one of six 737-300s in the company's fleet. This aircraft has been retrofitted with winglets that help reduce fuel consumption. (Christian Herbert Schöpf)

Cayman Airways, the flag carrier of the Cayman Islands, was founded in 1968 and operates a fleet that consists of a combination of jet and propeller-driven aircraft. This 737-3Q8 is one of the airline's four 737-300s which serve the international medium-haul routes connecting the island nation to the United States, Cuba, Honduras, and Jamaica. (Denis Desmon)

Founded in 1978, Germany's second largest airline, Air Berlin focuses on business traffic to major German and European cities. This 737-322 wears the livery used from the airline's founding until 2007. (Erik Johannesson)

The 737 has power receptacles on the starboard side of the nose to provide power when the engines and APU are shut off. To save costs, some operators use the gate's power supply, rather than an APU, to start the engines. (Robert W. Tidwell)

The 737, like many other commercial aircraft, uses an external air conditioning unit when parked at a terminal gate. The yellow hose attaches to the air conditioning connection on the underside of the fuselage. Often, the external air conditioning unit is part of the jetbridge. The internal air conditioning packs are located in the underside of the aircraft in front of the main gear wells. (Robert W. Tidwell)

Olympic Airways was sold to Artistotle Onassis shortly after it was founded in 1957. Onassis sold his shares to the Greek government in 1973. Olympic used 737-300s such as this 737-3Q8 for their medium-haul intercontinental routes. This aircraft was sold to Ryanair of Ireland after Olympic airlines was liquidated in 2009. (Malcom Nason)

Air China is a state-owned airline and the second largest airline in China. The airline operates a mix of Airbus and Boeing aircraft that service domestic and international routes. This 737-3J6 is part of the airline's fleet of 29 737-300s. (Denis Desmond)

Atlant-Soyuz is owned by private investors and the city of Moscow. The airline flies domestic and international routes mostly in Eastern Europe and some former Soviet republics. This 737-347 is one of the airline's two 737-300s. (Christian Herbert Schöpf)

One of the features that attracted customers early on was the seating layout of the 737. The six-abreast seating and acceptable seat pitch provided adequate comfort for passengers and helped airlines make the most of their short and medium routes. (Christopher Iwane)

Norwegian Air Shuttle, known simply as Norwegian, is the second largest airline in Scandinavia. The low-cost airline operates 27 737-300s such as this 737-36N. This is example is one of the "hero" aircraft which bears the image of a famous Norwegian on the vertical stabilizer. (Christian Herbert Schöpf)

Air Atlantis was a charter airline owned by TAP-Air Portugal. The airline started with a 707 and a 737-200. Eventually, the 737-200s were replaced with -300s such as this 737-3K2. (Trevor Hall)

This Lufthansa 737-330 is one of 10 737-300s that the airline bought during latter half of the 1980s as part of a modernization program that included orders for new 747s and Airbus widebodies. (Christopher Iwane)

At one time, this 737-3Q8 was the sole 737 that Air Vanuatu had in its fleet. The airline's lone 737 flew 16 hours per day, six says per week. The airline has recently replaced their 737-300 with a 737-800. (Phillip Capper)

Belavia, founded in 1996, is the flag carrier for the nation of Belarus. Belavia purchased three 737-3Q8 aircraft to replace many of their aging former Aeroflot Tu-154 airliners. The -300's seating capacity was greater than that of Belavia's Tu-154s which were configured for 131 seats. (Denis Desmond)

When the CFM56 engine was chosen as the powerplant for the -300, Boeing's engineers had to redesign the attachment system and the engine casing to guarantee sufficient ground clearance. Starting with the -300, engines were mounted on a pylon that wraps around the leading edge of the wing. (Robert W. Tidwell)

Southwest Airlines is the largest operator of 737-300s and one of the earliest customers for the type. This 737-3H4 is one of 173 in the airline's current fleet of 544 737s. (Robert W. Tidwell)

The 737-300s of Aloha Airlines endured some of the highest cycle rates in the industry because of the short sectors that the airline flies among the islands. (Savvas Garozis)

United Airlines operated 737-300s along with -200s and -500s until 2009. For many years, United had the second largest fleet of 737-300s. Some of the 737s were operated as part of airline's United Shuttle service while others flew in the airline's main routes. (Denis Desmond)

Freedom Air was Air New Zealand's low-cost airline. The company had five 737-300s in the fleet. The airline used aircraft such as this 737-33R in the domestic trunk routes. (Phillip Capper)

Shenzhen Airlines is a domestic and international airline based at Shenzhen Bao'an International Airport, China. The airline operates a mix of Boeing and Airbus aircraft, including eight 737-300s for domestic routes. (Savvas Garozis)

Boeing 737-400

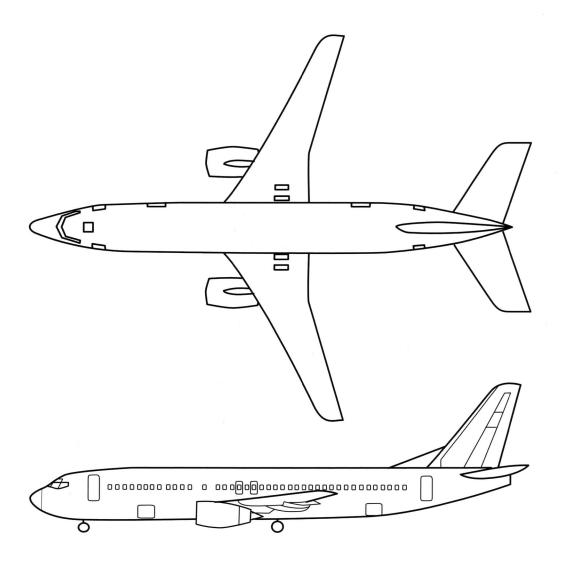

Production:	489
Passengers:	3-Class – N/A
	2-Class – 146
	1-Class - 168
Cargo:	1,373 cubic feet (38.9 cu m)
Engine:	CFM56-3B-2
	CFM56-3C
Maximum Thrust:	22,000 lbs (97.9 kN)
	23,500 lbs (104.5 kN)
Maximum Fuel Capacity:	6,311 gals (23,890 liters)
Maximum Takeoff Weight:	150,000 lbs (68,260kg)
Maximum Range:	2,160 naut. miles (4,000km)
Typical Cruise Speed:	Mach 0.745
Wingspan	94 feet 9 inches (28.9m)
Overall Length:	119 feet 7 inches (36.4m)
Tail Height:	36 feet 6 inches (11.1m)

737-400

Eager to build on the success of the -300, Boeing announced in June 1986 that the company would be turning out a stretched version of the -300. The company envisioned the -400 as a 150-seat class replacement for the 727. The aircraft was also intended to fill the gap between the 737-300 and the 757. Aside from the 10-foot stretch, the overall aircraft dimensions remained the same, greatly benefitting customers who already operated the -300.

To cope with the increased gross weight of the -400, Boeing chose the more powerful CFM56-3B-2 and CFM56-3C-1 engines. Another novelty on the -400 was was the bumper fitted on the tail to protect it from damage in the event of over rotation on takeoff. The -400SF freighter conversion can carry nine pallets of cargo (other conversions can accommodate 10 pallets). The -400SP (Special Performance) is equipped with winglets.

The stretch allowed the -400 to carry 146 passengers in a mixed configuration or up to 170 passengers in an all-economy configuration. The additional passenger capacity made it necessary to add another pair of overwing exits in order to conform to aviation safety requirements. The wing spar was strengthened in order to cope with the increased gross weight. In addition, an additional spoiler was added to each wing in order to improve deceleration. The -400 features a standard glass cockpit with an arrangement similar to that of the 757 and 767; however, the similarities are not enough to allow for common type rating with the 757 or 767. The 737-400, which rolled out on the same day as the 747-400, first took to the air on 19 February 1988 and two -400s were used in the seven-month flight-test program to attain FAA certification. The standard Maximum Take-off Weight of the -400 is 143,500 pounds, but the High Gross Weight version tips the scales at 150,000 pounds.

The large circular openings in front of the wheel wells on the -400 are the avionics bay vents. Boeing developed the -400 to occupy a niche between the 737-300 and the 757. The -400 is 10 feet longer than its predecessor and has a capacity of 170 passengers. (Monty Nicol)

This 737-429 is part of the Xtra Airways fleet, which is a mix of 737-400 and -800 aircraft. Xtra, formerly known as Casino Express, is a charter airline based in Boise, Idaho, that has on occasion leased aircraft to other airlines. (Denis Desmond)

AeroSvit, one of Ukraine's two flag carriers, was formed in 1994 with dry-leased 737-200s. It later expanded to a fleet of 17 aircraft, including Antonovs, SAABs, and Boeings like this 737-448. (Christian Herbert Schöpf)

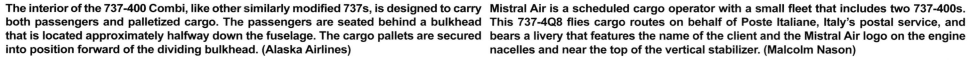

The interior of the 737-400 Combi, like other similarly modified 737s, is designed to carry both passengers and palletized cargo. The passengers are seated behind a bulkhead that is located approximately halfway down the fuselage. The cargo pallets are secured into position forward of the dividing bulkhead. (Alaska Airlines)

This 737-400 with the registration N765TA flies for the US Justice Department as part of the Justice Prisoner and Alien Transport System, JPATS, which transports prisoners and criminal aliens across the country. (Rick Schlamp)

Mistral Air is a scheduled cargo operator with a small fleet that includes two 737-400s. This 737-4Q8 flies cargo routes on behalf of Poste Italiane, Italy's postal service, and bears a livery that features the name of the client and the Mistral Air logo on the engine nacelles and near the top of the vertical stabilizer. (Malcolm Nason)

A 737-4H6, one of Malaysia Airlines' 37 737-400s, makes its approach to Tân Sơn Nhất International Airport, Hồ Chí Minh City, Vietnam. As of 2010, Malaysia Airlines, the Malaysian flag carrier, operated a fleet of 82 aircraft. (Huan Duong)

Qunatas Airways Limited is the world's oldest continuously operating airline. The airline currently flies a blend of Airbus and Boeing aircraft, including this 737-476 that displays the current Quantas livery. The Flying Kangaroo on the vertical stabilizer has been a part of the airline's livery since 1944. (Christoper Iwane)

This British Airways 737-436 features an Egyptian motif. The two Arabic words written on the nose translate as "Crossing Borders." Between 1997 and 2001 British Airways decorated 170 of its aircraft using ethnic themes related to countries that the airline served. (Phillip Capper)

Aircraft belonging to Piedmont Airlines, which was the launch customer for the -400, became part of the US Air fleet after that company acquired Piedmont. This US Airways 737-401 was ordered by Piedmont Airlines but it never wore Piedmont's livery prior to US Air's acquisition of the airline. (Christopher Iwane)

Blue Air is a small low-cost Romanian airline with a mixed fleet of 737s including this 737-4C9. Founded in 2004 and based in Bucharest, Blue Air operates mostly out of Aurel Vlaicu International Airport and services more than 20 destinatons, including many European cities outside Romania. (Erik Johannesson)

The main gear well of the 737 is a maze of hydraulic lines, power cables, and actuators. The metal screen panels at left in the photograph are protective screens that protect sensitive hydraulic systems from debris in the event of a tire blowout at altitude. (Chris Brady)

The lengthened fuselage and expanded passenger capacity of the -400 necessitated additional exits. There are two emergency exit doors on both sides of the aircraft at the mid-fuselage point. The emergency exit doors are outlined in gray on this US Airways 737-401. (Christopher Iwane)

The fact that the 737-400 fuselage is 10 feet longer than the -300 fuselage raised concerns that pilots might over-rotate on takeoff and damage the underside of the aft fuselage. Boeing therefore installed a tailskid on the underside of the empennage. The tailskid is visible as a bump just below the cheatline on this KLM 737-4Y0. (Christopher Iwane)

In 2004, the České Státní Aerolinie (ČSA), the Czech state airline, acquired four Boeing 737-400s. This 737-45S wears the livery the airline used until 2007. Founded in 1923, ČSA has a fleet of 38 aircraft, including eight 737s. (Phillip Capper)

Air UK Leisure was a short-lived charter service operated by Air UK. The airline was founded in 1987 and served as the first European customer for the 737-400. This 737-4Y0 was one of the seven -400s that the airline operated before shuttering in 1996. All of the airline's -400s were eventually transferred to KLM. (Axel Juengerich)

Icelandair, the national carrier of Iceland, acquired its first -400s in 1989 when there was a flurry of orders for the aircraft. The airline used -400s like this 737-408 on routes linking Iceland with Europe. The airline later replaced its 737s with 757s. (Axel Juengerich)

Tailwind, a Turkish charter airline founded as a British-Turkish joint venture in 2006, operates five wet-leased -400s like this 737-4Q8. The airline says that it chose the 737 based on the aircraft's record of safety and economy. (Axel Juengerich)

LOT, the Polish flag carrier, operates both the 737-400 and -500. This 737-45D is one of eight -400s in the fleet, four of which are flown on a charter basis. (Axel Juengerich)

Calima Aviacion is a Spanish charter that started operations in 2009. The airline consists of three -400s like this 737-448. All of their aircraft came from the Ukrainian AeroSvit fleet. (Alain Durand)

A loyal Boeing customer, Alaska Airlines operates many types of 737, including the 737-400 Combi, which helps the airline maximize earnings by carrying freight in the forward half of the fuselage and passengers in the aft half. (Alaska Air)

The 737, like many commercial aircraft, includes additional means to verify that the landing gear are down and locked. In the event that the landing gear indicator lights on the instrument panel malfunction, a member of the flight or cabin crew can use inspection windows to confirm that the landing gears are down and locked. (Bill Abbott)

The 737 features spoilers on the upper surface of the wing in front of its flaps. The numbers of spoilers varies among the versions. The 737-300 has one more flight spoiler on each wing than do the -100 and -200. Ground spoilers and flight spoilers on this aircraft deploy in combination with the flaps during landing. (Shane Bennett)

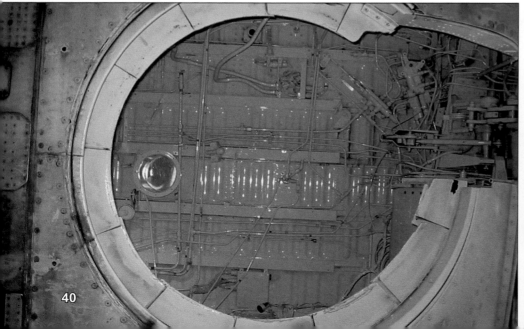

Iberia was one of many European operators for the 737-400. The airline leased aircraft such as this 737-4Y0 from another Spanish airline, Air Europa. (Alain Durand)

Brussels Airlines operates a mixed fleet of 49 aircraft, nine of wich are 737s. The airline's 737-300s and -400s are used on the airline's European routes. The airline's -400s are configured for 164 passengers. (Savvas Garozis)

JAL Express started operations in 1998 as Japan Airlines' low-cost subsidiary. The airline started operations with the 737-400. The airline still uses seven -400s on domestic routes. (Savvas Garozis)

Thai Airways International took delivery of its first -400 in 1990. This 737-4D7 bears the livery worn from 1974 to 2005. (Savvas Garozis)

Auxiliary Power Unit (APU) is located in a space in the tailcone of the empennage. The APU is a small gas turbine that drives a generator to provide electrical power to start the engines. The APU has its own fuel supply. The intake for the APU is on the starboard side of the empennage and the exhaust is in the tip of the tailcone. (Chris Brady)

A LOT 737-45D undergoes maintenance. Visible under the lifted nose cone is the 737's weather radar. The port engine has been removed and the engine pylon and mounting system are visible. The plastic covering for the interior of the forward passenger door has been removed, revealing the metal structure of the door. (Piotr Bozyk)

İstanbul Airlines, founded in 1985, operated a dozen 737-400s before ceasing operations in the year 2000. This 737-4Y0 was originally ordered by the large, ill-fated aircraft leasing company Guinness Peat Aviation Group, PLC. (Trevor Hall)

With a range of 1,960 nautical miles, the -400 afforded low-cost and tourist airlines with an affordable means of making continental flights. Futura Airlines of Spain used their 737-4Y0 aircraft to reach destinations throughout Europe. (Trevor Hall)

Boeing 737-500

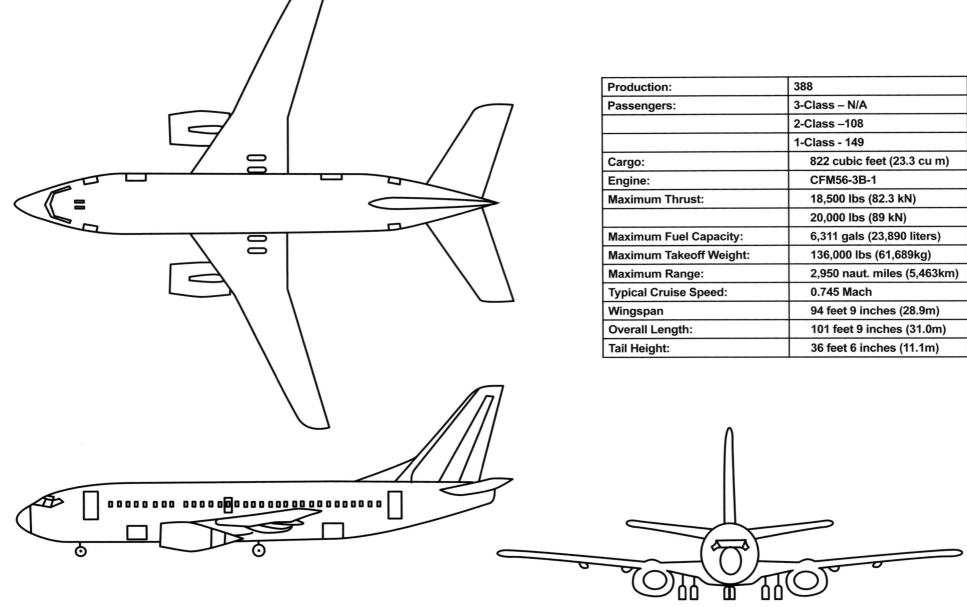

Production:	388
Passengers:	3-Class – N/A
	2-Class –108
	1-Class - 149
Cargo:	822 cubic feet (23.3 cu m)
Engine:	CFM56-3B-1
Maximum Thrust:	18,500 lbs (82.3 kN)
	20,000 lbs (89 kN)
Maximum Fuel Capacity:	6,311 gals (23,890 liters)
Maximum Takeoff Weight:	136,000 lbs (61,689kg)
Maximum Range:	2,950 naut. miles (5,463km)
Typical Cruise Speed:	0.745 Mach
Wingspan	94 feet 9 inches (28.9m)
Overall Length:	101 feet 9 inches (31.0m)
Tail Height:	36 feet 6 inches (11.1m)

737-500

The 737-500 is the shortest and last of the second generation 737s. When Boeing introduced the -300 to the market, the aircraft was intended to supplement rather than directly replace the -200. However, the -300 and its immediate successor were both longer than the -200. Boeing noted that many -200 customers were merely interested in a more efficient replacement for the -200; thus, the -500 was born. The -500 measures 101 ft 9 in while the -200 measures 100 ft 2 in. The -500 also enjoys a high degree of parts commonality with the -300 and -400. The aircraft is powered by a choice of two CFM engines. The standard -500 uses 18,500-lb thrust CFM56-3B-1 engines while the high gross weight version uses the 20,000-lb thrust CFM56-3C-1 engines.

At first, Boeing considered designating the series as the -1000 or the 737 Lite, but it was decided that -500 was a much more logical choice. Boeing offered customers a choice of cockpits: a more traditional electromechanical arrangement or an electronic "glass cockpit." The -200 ceased production in August of 1988, but the -500 was ready to take up the slack with its first flight on 30 June 1989. Only one aircraft was used in the seven month long flight certification tests. The -500 offers an aircraft comparable in dimensions to the -200, but with a 25% improvement in efficiency.

Rossiya is a charter airline that also operates VIP flights on behalf of the Russian Government including flights for the President of Russia. This 737-548 is one of five -500s that the airline operates in its commercial fleet. (Christian Herbert Schöpf)

The -500 was designed with -200 customers in mind. The idea was to provide the advantages of the 737-300 with dimensions close to those of the -200. Sales were slow in the United States, but overseas sales were good. Czech Airlines was among the first Eastern European airlines to purchase the type. This 737-55S joined Czech Airlines in the early 1990s. (Christian Herbert Schöpf)

Ukraine International Airlines is the flag carrier of Ukraine and operates an all-737 fleet. This 737-5Y0 is one of five -500s in a fleet of 19 aircraft. The aircraft leasing company GPA Group originally ordered this aircraft. From this angle, it is easy to see the triple slotted flaps and the pointed afterbodies for the flap track fairings. The afterbodies were altered in the Next Generation 737s. (Christian Herbert Schöpf)

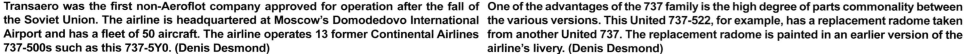

Transaero was the first non-Aeroflot company approved for operation after the fall of the Soviet Union. The airline is headquartered at Moscow's Domodedovo International Airport and has a fleet of 50 aircraft. The airline operates 13 former Continental Airlines 737-500s such as this 737-5Y0. (Denis Desmond)

One of the advantages of the 737 family is the high degree of parts commonality between the various versions. This United 737-522, for example, has a replacement radome taken from another United 737. The replacement radome is painted in an earlier version of the airline's livery. (Denis Desmond)

A scene that passengers hope to never see – emergency oxygen masks deployed from the PSU. The PSU has enough oxygen for 12 minutes; this is based on the time needed for a controlled descent from 37,000 feet to 14,000 feet, and then from 14,000 feet to 10,000 feet. (Chris Brady)

BMIbaby is a low-cost subsidiary of British Midland International and provides flights to Europe from the airline's four bases in the United Kingdom. The bulk of the airline's fleet is 737-300s, but the airline also operates three 737-500s including this 737-5Q8. (Christopher Iwane)

Air Nippon is a regional airline and subsidiary of All Nippon Airways. Air Nippon is one of the few Japanese operators of the -500. This 737-54K has the distinction of being the last 500 made. (Erik Johannesson)

Lufthansa was among the earliest European customers for the 737-500 and received their order for 30 of the aircraft within a year. The airline operates the -500s in their medium-haul fleet. (Christian Herbert Schöpf)

LOT Polish Airlines was part of a second wave of customers that ordered the -500 for their fleets. These orders were part of a modernization program to replace aging Soviet civil aircraft. This 737-55D bears the Star Alliance logo; LOT joined the alliance in 2003. (Erik Johannesson)

Bulgaria Air is the flag carrier and successor for Bulgaria's Balkan Bulgarian Airlines. There were three 737-500s in Balkan Bulgarian Airline's fleet, but this 737-522 was purchased from United Airlines. The -500 affords good performance for routes up to 1,520nm and provides a competitive take-off weight for its class. (Christopher Iwane)

Pulkovo was a state-owned Soviet airline which remained in government hands after the fall of the Soviet Union. The airline was merged with Rossiya in 2006. Pulkovo's five 737-500 airliners were transferred to Rossiya as part of the merger. (Savvas Garozis)

This 737-5H6 was the sole -500 operated by the Nigerian airline Air Midwest, but it was returned to its lessor in 2010. The aircraft had been previously operated by British Airways, Malaysia Airlines, and Jet Airways. (Malcom Nason)

This 737-5H4 is one of the 25 -500s that the airline ordered. These aircraft have taken over many of the routes once served by the airline's -200s. (Robert W. Tidwell)

Estonian Air, the flag carrier for Estonia, operates a total of five aircraft including three 737-500. The airline leases all of its aircraft. (Savvas Garozis)

The -500 has been well received in Asia in terms of the number of customers ordering the aircraft. China Southern placed the most initial orders for the 737-500 in China. (Savvas Garozis)

Braathens SAFE ordered both -400s and -500s in close succession. The aircraft that the airline ordered were equipped with glass cockpits in which much of the instrumentation was replaced with multifunction video displays. (Savvas Garozis)

SABENA, the former national airline of Belgium, ordered their -500s in the early 1990s. The airline ordered six -500s. Also in the early 1990s, the Belgian government greatly reduced its ownership stake in the airline and led it on the path to privatization. (Savvas Garozis)

Royal Air Maroc has a long history with the 737 starting with the -200. As of 2010, six aircraft of the airline's fleet of 737s are 737-500s. These aircraft are used primarily on the RAM's European routes. RAM received this aircraft from Boring in 1997 and continues in service with the airline. (Savvas Garozis)

Airzena, a private airline in the Republic of Georgia, got its start as a charter service. In early 2000, the airline launched a Westernization scheme by leasing two 737-500s from Hapag-Lloyd. This 737-59D, 4L-TGR, served with a number of airlines before joining the Airzena fleet. The aircraft was delivered to Linjeflyg in 1990 before becoming part of the SAS fleet. After serving with a few British carriers, Airzena purchased the plane in 2008. This aircraft has retained the "eyebrow" windows above the cockpit windows. This is a feature of the 707 forward fuselage on which the 737 fuselage is based and offered a better view of the night sky in the event pilots needed to use celestial navigation. (Axel Juengerich)

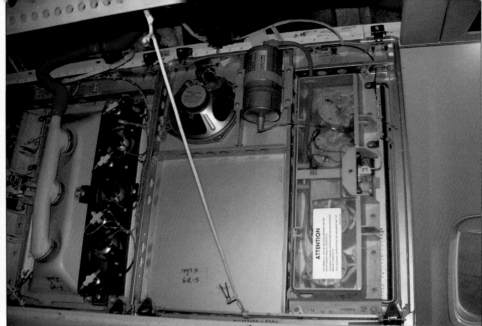

In the years before its demise, Lithuanian Air Lines tried to create a more modern image. This 737-522 wears the bright livery that the airline used from 2007 onward when it was rebranded as FlyLAL. The airline ceased operations in 2009. (Phillip Capper)

Sky Europe was a low-cost Slovakian airline that operated an all-737 fleet. The airline operated two 737-500s. These aircraft were dry-leased from Avia Asset Management. The airline flew charter and scheduled passenger short-haul routes. (Savvas Garozis)

The Passenger Service Unit (PSU) is the panel that passengers see above their seat. The PSU includes air vents, reading lamps, flight attendant call buttons, and the emergency oxygen masks. The yellow objects are the emergency oxygen masks and the oxygen supply comes from the silver canister marked with a dark yellow band. (Chris Brady)

Continental Airlines was one of the first U.S. carriers to order the 737-500. The airline currently operates 39 of the type on domestic medium-haul routes. (Christopher Iwane)

From 1990 to 2005, Aer Lingus operated 10 737-500s such as this 737-548 in the airline's domestic and European routes. When Aer Lingus became an all-Airbus fleet, many of the airline's 737-500s were sold to Russian and Eastern European airlines. This aircraft became part of the Air Baltic fleet. The articulated flap track fairings are visible from this angle; the fairings retain the pointed afterbodies found on earlier 737s. The flaptrack fairings and afterbodies were altered in the -600 and had a less pointed design. This aircraft has flaps and leading edge slats set for approach. From this angle, the articulation of the flap track fairings is clearly visible. The fairings terminate in a pointed afterbody whereas later models of the 737 feature a blunt afterbody. The Krueger flaps, inboard of the engines, are not visible on this aircraft at this angle. (Axel Juengerich)

SmartWings flies a fleet of 24 aircraft, but only owns two aircraft, both of which are 737-500s. The -500s are configured for all-economy seating and bear the SmartWings livery, whereas the leased leased aircraft do not. (Savvas Garozis)

Hokkaido International Airlines is a low-cost airline that connects the cities on the Japanese island of Hokkaido with the island of Honshu via Tokyo. The -500 forms the backbone of the airline's small fleet. (Savvas Garozis)

The -500 is well-suited for airlines that have routes longer than the -200 can handle but where passenger demand does not require a significantly larger aircraft. Garuda Indonesia has a number of domestic and regional routes for which the -500 is ideal. (Savvas Garozis)

The 737-500 provides an economical means for Aeroflot Don, a low-cost Russian airline, to serve destinations in Russia, Europe, Asia, and Africa. (Savvas Garozis)

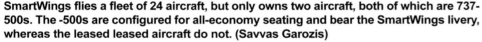

Orenair, Orenburg Airlines, was formed in 1932 as a division of Aeroflot, but the airline has operated under its own name beginning since 1992. The airline's fleet includes four -500s: two in single-class and two in two-class seating arrangements. (Savvas Garozis)

SAS, the largest airline in Scandinavia, serves as the flag carrier for Sweden, Norway, and Denmark. The airlines uses their 737s, including eight -500s, to serve European routes. (Denis Desmond)

This 737-529 belongs to the Serbian charter airline Aviogenex. The aircraft, operating under the name "Kon Tiki Sky," is flown on a wet-lease basis for MAT Macedonian Airlines. (Denis Desmond)

Egyptair is the state-owned airline of Egypt and operates routes in Egypt, Africa, Asia, Europe, and the Americas. This 737-566 is one of the four -500 that the airline operates. (Trevor Hall)

Boeing 737-600

Production:	68
Passengers:	3-Class – N/A
	2-Class – 110
	1-Class - 132
Cargo:	720 cubic feet (20.4 cu m)
Engine:	CFM56-7B-18
	CFM56-7B-22 High Gross Weight
Maximum Thrust:	19,500 lbs (86.7 kN)
	22,700 lbs (101 kN)
Maximum Fuel Capacity:	6,875 U.S. gals (26,025 liters)
Maximum Takeoff Weight:	144,500 lbs (65,544kg)
Maximum Range:	1,340 naut. miles (2,481km)
	3,050 naut. miles (5,649km) HGW version
	3,225 naut. miles (5,973km) 2-class w/winglets
Typical Cruise Speed:	Mach 0.785
Wingspan	112 feet 7 inches (34.3m)
Overall Length:	102 feet 6 inches (31.2m)
Tail Height:	41 feet 2 inches (12.5m)

737-600

The -600 is the first of the Next Generation 737s and, along with the -700, is one of the smaller members of the Next Generation aircraft. The -600 measures 102ft 6in and seats 110 passengers in a two class configuration or 132 passengers in a single class configuration. The -600's wing has a greater chord and span which results in a 25% greater wing area over the previous models. The -600 uses 19,500-lb thrust CFM56-7B-18 engines in the standard version and 22,700-lb thrust CFM56-7B-22s in the high gross weigh versions. The CFM56-7 series of engines consist of the core of the CFM56-5 coupled with the CFM56-3's low pressure compressor and a 61in fan. The more powerful engines and improved wings allow the aircraft to cruise at .785 Mach. Also, the larger wings allow for greater fuel capacity which provides the NG aircraft with transcontinental range. The powerful engines and the improved wing allow the -600 to have a maximum take-off weight (MTOW) of 124,000 lbs and the high gross-weight versions have a MTOW of 143,500 lbs. The -600 can carry 110 passengers to a range of 1,340 nautical miles. The NG aircraft feature some other refinements such as a flight deck derived from the 777 with six flat panel displays. Moreover, the NG aircraft have 33% fewer parts compared with the Classic 737s and the NGs have a single moving assembly line which helps to speed production. Only 68 -600s have been built.

This T737-6H3 is one of the -600s that Tunisair ordered from Boeing. Most of the -600s have remained with the original operators while some have been either retired or sold to governments or private corporations. (Christian Herbert Schöpf)

Founded in 1996, West Jet is a Canadian low-cost airline that provides charter and scheduled flights to destinations in Canada, the United States, Mexico, and the Caribbean. The airline operates an all-737 fleet of 88 aircraft. This 737-6CT is one of 13 -600s in the fleet. All aircraft feature leather seats and seatback televisions. (Denis Desmond)

The 737-600 marked the start of the Next Generation 737s. Beginning with design of the -600, the 737 enjoyed an updated wing design that provided 25% more wing area and 30% more fuel capacity than previous versions of the 737. The Next Generation 737s also feature a vertical stabilizer that is 4 feet, 8 inches taller than those on the 737-300, -400, and -500. (Savvas Garozis)

Some airlines, such as Malev Hungarian Airlines, used the -600 to replace or augment the -500s in their fleets. The -600 provided seating capacity similar to that of its predecessor, but with longer range and better overall performance. (Erik Johannesson)

The -600 provided airlines like Austria's Lauda Air with a great deal of flexibility. European low-cost and tourist airlines, with seating that can range from 108 to 132, can reach all of Europe, North Africa, and the Middle East. The CFM56-7B18 engines of the -600 were derated to 19,500 lbs, but provided a range of 1,340 nautical miles. (Axel Juengerich)

In recent years, "Janet Jet," the U.S. DoD airline that shuttles personnel to and from Groom Lake, replaced its 737-200s with 737-600s such as this former China Southwest Airlines 737-66N. Unlike previous "Janet" aircraft, this aircraft is registered to the Department of the Air Force. (Cameron Jones)

When Lauda Air became a subsidiary of Austrian Airlines, most of Lauda's fleet was absorbed into that of Austrian Airlines. This 737-6Z9 is one of the former Lauda aircraft. (Gerald Fischer)

The production run for the -600 was among the lowest in the 737 family. Only a handful of airlines purchased -600s when the series was introduced in 1998. The bulk of the -600 production was purchased by large airlines. (Axel Junegerich)

Boeing 737-700

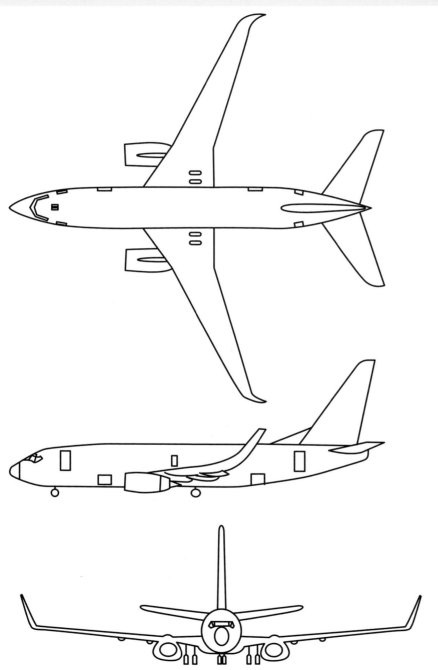

Production:	883 ordered
Passengers:	3-Class – N/A
	2-Class – 128
	1-Class – 148 (140 in -700C)
Cargo:	966 cubic feet (27.4 cu m)
	966 cubic feet (27.4 cu m) No aux. tanks -700ER
	165 cubic feet (4.7 cu m) 9 aux. tanks -700ER
	966 cubic feet (27.3 cu m) -700C
Engine:	CFM56-7B-20
	CFM56-7B-22
Maximum Thrust:	20,600 lbs (91.6 kN)
	22,700 lbs (101 kN)
	24,200 lbs (107.6 kN) High Gross Weight versions
	26,300 lbs (117 kN) -700ER
	27,300 lbs (121.4 kN) -700C
Maximum Fuel Capacity:	6,875 U.S. gals (26,025 liters)
Maximum Takeoff Weight:	154,500 lbs (70,080kg)
	171,000 lbs (77,565kg) -700ER/-700C
Maximum Range:	3,440 naut. miles (6,371km) [2-class with winglets]
	5,775 naut. miles (10,695km) [1-class with 9 aux fuel tanks and winglets] -700ER
	3,285 naut. miles (6,084km) [Passenger 1-Class] -700C
	3,000 naut. miles (5,556km) [Cargo] -700C
Typical Cruise Speed:	Mach 0.785
Wingspan	112 feet 7 inches (34.3m)
	117 feet 5 inches (35.8m) with winglets
Overall Length:	110 feet 4 inches (33.6m)
Tail Height:	41 ft 2 in (12.5 m)

737-700

The 737-700 was the first Next Generation 737 developed despite numerically following the -600. The first -700 rolled off the production line on 8 December 1996. Three aircraft were used in the test and certification flights.

The -700 measures 110ft 4in in length and can carry 128 passengers in a two-class configuration or 148 passengers in a single-seat configuration. The standard -700 is equipped with CFM56-7B-22s rated at 20,600 lbs of thrust and the high gross weight version is equipped with the 22,700-lb thrust CFM56-7B-24s. The -700 has replaced the -300 in Boeing's commercial lineup and serves as a direct competitor with the Airbus A319.

The cargo version, -700C, carries over 41,400 lbs of cargo on eight pallets. The -700QC (Quick Change) version has pallet-mounted seats to allow for a rapid transition from cargo to passenger service or vice versa. The -700C and -700QC also feature strengthened wings similar to those in the 737 BBJ. In an all-passenger layout, the aircraft can carry up to 140 passengers in a single-class configuration or 120 passengers in a mixed-class configuration. In an all-cargo layout, the aircraft can carry up to 40,000 pounds of cargo up to 2,880 nautical miles. The military transport version is the C-40.

On 31 January 2006, Boeing launched the -700ER with All Nippon Airways as the launch customer. This version of the -700 drew inspiration from the BBJ and has the longest range of any 737 (5,630nm). There is a high performance option for the -700ER which can accommodate up to nine auxiliary fuel tanks, providing a maximum fuel load of 10,707 gallons of fuel.

AeroMexico, the flag carrier for Mexico, operates a fleet of 93 aircraft ranging from small regional jets to Boeing 777s. The airline operates 28 737-700s on their short and medium-haul routes. As of 2010, the airline has pending orders for another 10 -700s. (Denis Desmond)

There are separate doors for the fore and aft baggage holds. The access doors are hinged at the top and open inwards. The 737 is low enough to the ground that ground crews can load baggage into the holds without equipment. Conveyors, such as the one in this photograph, are used to make loading and unloading baggage more efficient. (Robert W. Tidwell)

Hamburg International was an independent passenger airline that operated charter services for European tour operators. The airline's fleet consisted of nine leased aircraft. This was the sole 737-700 in the fleet. (Denis Desmond)

Aerolineas Argentinas is the flag carrier of Argentina and the nation's largest airline and operates a mix of Boeing and Airbus aircraft. The airline decided to replace its aging 737-200s with -700s. This 737-76N is part of the replacement plan and previously flew with Sky Europe. (Malcolm Nason)

The -700 is nearly two feet shorter than the -600, but has a higher takeoff weight (133,000 lbs) than the -600 (124,000 lbs). The -700 also has a maximum range of 3,260 nautical miles. The -700 owes its improved performance to a pair of CFM-7B20 engines that produce 22,700 lbs of thrust, each. (Malcolm Nason)

Europe Airpost is an interesting French-based airline. By day, their fleet of 19 737s provides passenger service for airlines and tour companies. By night, some of their aircraft carry mail and parcels for the postal service. This 737-73V is one of a small number of aircraft in the fleet that provide only passenger service. (Malcolm Nason)

Aloha Airlines concentrated on flights among the Hawaiian Islands during most of the airline's history. There had been some attempts in the 1980s to provide routes outside the islands, but they were short lived. Beginning in 2000, Aloha offered routes to the US mainland with their newly acquired 737-700s. (Denis Desmond)

Southwest Airlines was the launch customer for the -700. This 737-7H4 "The Herbert D. Kelleher" is named in honor of the airline's co-founder. As of 2010, the airline operates 350 -700s in its all-737 fleet of 550 aircraft. (Denis Desmond)

Boeing introduced "glass cockpits" in 737s with some of the -300s. The cockpit of the 737 has become increasingly computerized with each Next Generation series of the aircraft, as this -700 demonstrates. In spite of the presence of large electronic displays, the Next Generation aircraft retain a few analog instruments that serve as as backups. (Bill Shemley)

The wing of the 737 has retained the same basic shape over the years, but has been stretched and refined from one generation to the next. One feature of Next Generation aircraft (-600 onward) was the flap track fairing (the red elongated structures on the underside of the wing). In earlier versions, the fairings had a more rounded cross section. (Robert W. Tidwell)

The horizontal stabilizer trim for the 737 is controlled by adjusting the angle of attack of the entire stabilizer. The three white hash marks near the root of the stabilizer mark different trim settings. This feature of the 737 allows the pilot to control pitch by adjusting the stabilizer trim in the event that the elevators malfunction. (Robert W. Tidwell)

This 737-700C interior shows what is possible in the combi configuration. Owned by a charter service that caters to upmarket clients, the aircraft features four abreast first class seats with greater seat pitch than is used in economy seating. (Jon Ostrower)

Winglets were introduced on the 737-800 and many airlines have been retrofitting some of their earlier-model 737s with winglets. However, many -700s such as this China Southern 737-7K9, continue to fly with conventional wingtips. (Rick Schlamp)

The Dutch low-cost airline Transavia provides scheduled and charter services to popular vacation destinations in Europe, Asia, and Africa. The airline operates a fleet that is a mix of 737-700 and -800 aircraft. This 737-7K2 was retrofitted with winglets in 2005. (Savvas Garozis)

Prior to the -600, the pitot tubes and airflow sensors were located below the rear-most cockpit window. In the Next Generation aircraft, these items were moved forward to a position below the front cockpit window. The 737-700C and -700QC air data probes are in the pre-Next Generation configuration. (Robert W. Tidwell)

The flight data probe arrangements for Next Generation 737s heark back to the -100 and -200 which had a single pitot tube on the port side of the nose. The object below the pitot tube is an airflow sensor. The starboard side of the nose has two pitot tubes with an airflow sensor below the bottom tube. (Robert W. Tidwell)

In spite of following the -600 numerically, the -700 was the first of the Next Generation 737s to fly. Regular versions of the -700 can fly up to 1,540 nautical miles while High Gross Weight versions can reach 3,260 nautical miles. These ranges allow the -700 and other Next Generation 737s to make transcontinental flights. (Denis Desmond)

Valves located on the empennage of the 737 regulate cabin pressure. The rectangular opening below the cabin service door is the Main Outflow Valve, which regulates cabin pressure by adjusting the outflow of cabin air. (Robert W. Tidwell)

Soon after winglets were introduced in the -800, Boeing made winglet retrofit kits available for certain earlier versions of the 737. This Kenyan Airlines aircraft was the first -700 to receive a winglet retrofit. (Rick Schlamp)

The 737-700C is the convertible version of the -700. The -700C can be converted from a passenger to a cargo configuration, and vice versa, fairly quickly. The Quick Change version uses pallet-mounted seats to make conversion easier. (Justin Pistone)

The pre-Next Generation 737s had a single static source on each side of the forward fuselage. The Next Generation 737s feature an additional static source on both sides of the forward fuselage just aft for the forward doors. (Robert W. Tidwell)

This -700 has been retrofitted with a transceiver for in-flight WiFi capability. The proliferation of personal WiFi-capable devices has prompted airlines to provide in-flight WiFi services. Newer 737s are being fitted with systems to provide these services. (Robert W. Tidwell)

Boeing 737-800

Production:	1,028 ordered
Passengers:	3-Class – 160
	2-Class – 184
	1-Class - 189
Cargo:	1,555 cubic feet (44 cu m)
Engine:	CFM56-7B-24
	CFM56-7B-27 for high gross weight versions
Maximum Thrust:	24,200 lbs (107.6 kN)
	27,300 lbs (121.4 kN)
Maximum Fuel Capacity:	6,875 U.S. gals (26,025 liters)
Maximum Takeoff Weight:	174,200 lbs (79,016kg)
Maximum Range:	3,115 nautical miles (5,769km) [2-class with winglets]
Typical Cruise Speed:	Mach 0.785
Wingspan without winglets	112 feet 7 inches (34.3m)
Wingspan with winglets	117 feet 5 inches (35.8m)
Overall Length:	129 feet 6 inches (39.5m)
Tail Height:	41 feet 2 inches (12.5m)

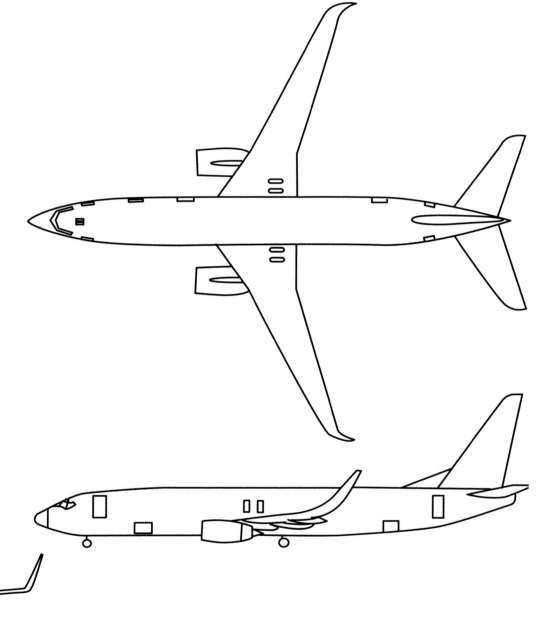

737-800

The -800, along with the -900, is one of the largest members of the 737 family. The -800 was launched in 1994 and features the same refinements as the earlier Next Generation aircraft. The -800 was originally known as the 737-400X Stretch within Boeing because the fuselage consisted, essentially, of a 9ft 9in stretch of the basic -400 fuselage (112ft 7in total length); the aircraft even has a tail bumper on the same fuselage frame section as the -400. The aircraft can accommodate as many as 162 passengers in a two-class arrangement or a maximum of 189 in a single-class arrangement with a 30-in pitch.

The aircraft also features an EFIS flightdeck similar to that of the 777 with six LCD displays for flight information. Like the -400, the -800 has two overwing exits on the left and right. The standard -800 is equipped with CFM56-7B-24 engines rated at 24,200 lbs of thrust and the high gross weight version uses CFM56-7B-27s rated at 27,300 lbs of thrust. The aircraft compares well against its competitors and has good fuel economy. For example, the -800 burns approximately 20% less fuel than an MD-80 on a comparable route.

The -800 has enjoyed strong sales since its launch and has been the highest selling Next Generation 737. The low-cost Irish airline Ryanair placed the largest single order for the aircraft with a firm order for over 100 airframes soon after the aircraft's launch. Ryanair is one of the largest operators of the -800 with a fleet of 300 of the aircraft. The -800 serves as a competitor with the A320. Moreover, the -800 serves as a replacement option for airlines operating 727-200s, MD-80s, and MD-90s. As of January 2011, Boeing has manufactured 2,135 -800s.

Continental Airlines operates 126 737-800s in its fleet of 607 aircraft. The -800 is powered by two CFM56-7B-26 high-bypass turbofans with a rated thrust of 26,300 pounds each. Many U.S. airlines acquired the -800 as a direct replacement for 727-200s in their fleets. (Continental Airlines)

Prior to its launch in September 1994, the -800 was known as the -400X Stretch. The -800 is 9 ft, 9 in longer than the -400. Although the two aircraft have a nearly identical maximum passenger capacity, the -800 has a much higher maximum range (2,940 nautical miles for high gross-weight versions). (Gerald Fischer)

This 737-8K5 is part of TUI Fly's fleet of 41 737s that provide charter and scheduled low-cost flights. TUI Fly was formed in 2007 from a fusion of Hapag-Lloyd Express and Hapag-Lloyd Flug. Like the -400s, the -800s have two over-wing exits on both sides. (Denis Desmond)

This Ryanair 737-8AS demonstrates a normal take-off rotation for a 737-800; however, the long fuselage of the -800 means that damage from over rotation is a possibility. To protect the underside of the empennage, Boeing added a bumper like those on the -400s to the underside of section 48 of the fuselage. (Christian Herbert Schöpf)

Winglets were introduced in the 737 family with the -800 in 2001. The winglets improve fuel efficiency by reducing aerodynamic drag. The winglets have helped reduce fuel consumption by as much as 7 percent. (Denis Desmond)

The -800 was designed as a stretched -400 and shares many similarities with the earlier aircraft. For example, the -800 has a tailskid and two over-wing exits on both sides of the fuselage. However, the -800 has significantly greater range and fuel economy than the -400. This Austrian Airlines -800, one of six in the airline's fleet, wears the striking new livery introduced in 2003. (Christian Herbert Schöpf)

The second -800 off the line was delivered to TUI Hapag-Lloyd. The airline was one of the later incarnations of Hapag-Lloyd airlines. (Savvas Garozis)

The complete modular units (seats, galleys, lavatories, etc.) come to the production line for installation, pre-finished in the customer's color scheme. (Jon Ostrower)

Hapag-Lloyd Express, previously branded as HLX.com, was a no-frills express airline that operated routes in Germany and to destinations in the rest of Europe. The airline painted aircraft such as this 737-8K5 to resemble a taxi in an effort support the idea that the airline offered inexpensive, reliable flights. (Malcolm Nason)

This Pacific Blue 737-8BK proves that nose art is not just for military aircraft. Many aircraft in the Pacific Blue fleet have their own individual nose art. (Christopher Iwane)

This Futura 737-800 operated for Funjet Vacations, an American tour/vacation package company. Futura provided similar package-tour companies with low-cost flights to popular holiday destinations in Europe. (Savvas Garozis)

Like other cabin furnishings, the seats arrive from suppliers prefinished, in the color scheme and material requested by the customer, and ready for installation. Other options such as in-flight entertainment systems also arrive preinstalled. (Jon Ostrower)

Air Vanuatu's fleet of 10 aircraft operates one jet. In the past, the sole jet aircraft was a 737-300 which served as the airline's flagship. In 2008, the airline replaced their workhorse -300 with this 737-800. (Phillip Capper)

The Czech carrier Travel Service Airlines operates 13 737-800s in its small fleet. The aircraft allow the airline to reach destinations in Europe, Africa, and Asia. The -800 is also popular with large European carriers that use the aircraft on many of their long range routes within the continent. (Savvas Garozis)

This 737-800 features the new design aesthetic that Boeing has developed for its commercial aircraft. The new interior features redesigned overhead lighting, Passenger Service unit panels, and overhead bins. Many later models also feature in-flight entertainment systems. (Jon Ostrower)

The cargo capacity of the 737 has grown greatly since the -100. The baggage hold of the 737-800 has a total volume of 1,555 cubic feet. The forward baggage hold alone has a volume of 672 cubic feet which is almost as large as the total baggage hold volume of a 737-600. (John T. Miller)

The 737 has developed a loyal following with many airlines. The nose of this Alaska Air 737-890 is a testament to the carrier's loyalty to Boeing commercial aviation. Of the airline's fleet of 112 aircraft, 55 are -800s. (Christopher Iwane)

The galley on the 737 features accommodations for storing and heating food as well as storage for the service carts under the counter. The red metal latches hold the carts in place when not in use. (Joe Nazarian).

The Austrain vacation and leisure airline Lauda Air operates seven 737-800s. The small fleet provides scheduled and charter services to 56 destinations in eight countries. Each of Lauda's aircraft are named for a famous musician, this aircraft is named "Miles Davis." (Christian Herbert Schöpf)

Sunexpress is owned by Turkish Airlines and Lufthansa. The airline started as a charter service linking Antlaya, Turkey, with Frankfurt, Germany. The airline's entire fleet of 25 aircraft consists of 737-800s. The aircraft are used to reach 82 destinations in Europe and Turkey. (Christian Herbert Schöpf)

Boeing 737-900

Production:	55 plus 165 orders for -900ER versions
Passengers:	3-Class – N/A
	2-Class – 177 (180 in -900ER)
	1-Class – 189 (215 in -900ER)
Cargo:	1,835 cubic feet (52 cu m)
	1,676 cubic feet (47.5 cu m) w/aux. tank
	1,587 cubic feet (44.9 cu m) w/2 aux. tanks
Engine:	CFM56-7B-26
	CFM56-7B-27 for High Gross Weight versions and -900ER
Maximum Thrust:	26,300 lbs (117 kN)
	27,300 lbs (121.4 kN) -900ER
Maximum Fuel Capacity:	6,878 gals (26,036 liters)
	7,837 gals (29,666 liters) -900ER
Maximum Takeoff Weight:	174,200 lbs (79,016kg)
	187,700 lbs (85,130kg) -900ER
Maximum Range:	2,458 naut. miles (4,552km)
	3,265 naut. miles (6,047km) -900ER in 2-class configuration with winglets and aux. tanks
Typical Cruise Speed:	Mach 0.785
Wingspan without winglets	112 feet 7 inches (34.3m)
Wingspan with winglets	117 feet 5 inches (35.8m)
Overall Length:	138 feet 2 inches (42.11m)
Tail Height:	41 feet 2 inches (12.5m)

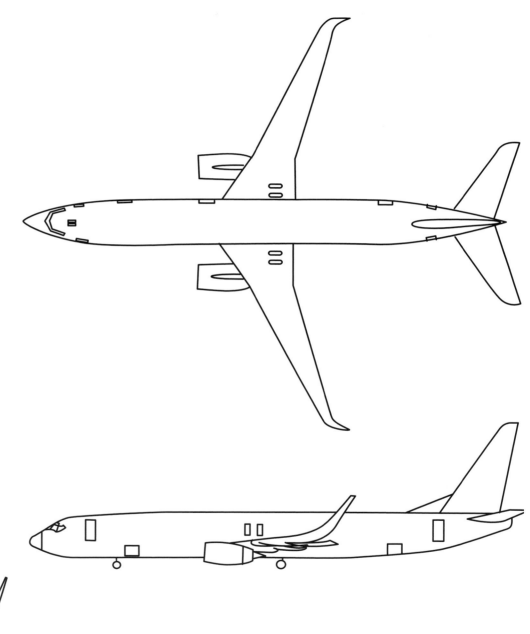

737-900

In April 1997, Boeing started work on the -900, which was meant to compete with the Airbus A321 in the 185-220 seat market. The -900 was launched on 10 September 1997 with Alaska Airlines placing the first 10 orders. The first flight was on 3 August 2000 and the first delivery was on 15 May 2001. The standard -900 flies with the 26,300-lb thrust CFM56-7B-26 engines. The high gross-weight version is equipped with the 27,300-lb thrust CFM56-7B-27. The -900 is the longest 737 to date, with a fuselage length of 138ft 2in. The wingspan and height are the same as the -800. The -900 can carry 177 passengers in a two-class configuration at a 36-inch pitch or 189 passengers at a 32-inch pitch. As of January 2011, a total of 52 -900s have been delivered.

The long-range, high-capacity version of the -900, the -900ER, was launched on 18 July 2005 with Indonesia's Lion Air as the launch partner. The improved capabilities of the aircraft are the result of refinements such as a flat rear pressure bulkhead, strengthened wings, and enhanced leading and trailing edge flap systems. The aircraft also features an adjustable tailskid and an additional pair of exit doors. The -900ER can carry 215 passengers (26 more than the standard -900) and has a range 500 nautical miles greater than a stock -900. The -900ER was developed to offer a direct competitor to the A321 and offer the range and passenger capacity of the 757-200. A -900ER can fly at a range of 3,200 nautical miles if it is equipped with auxiliary fuel tanks and optional blended winglets. The airfoil design of the -900ER allows it to cruise at .78 Mach (compared with .74 mach of earlier models) and make sprints up to .84 Mach. By 2011, the -900ER had become the standard for the -900 series.

To date, over 50 -900s have been built and delivered to a small number of customers. The -900 is the longest 737 and offers 9 percent more cabin space than the -800. The latest version of the 737 is close to the length of the 707-120. Alaska Airlines operates 12 -900s in its fleet of 112 737s. (Axel Juengerich)

Much has changed from the early days of civil aviation especially with respect to passenger convenience. The lavatories on earlier 737s were flush toilets that emptied the waste water into an internal storage tank. Later models such as the 737-900ER are equipped with vacuum toilets that also empty into a storage tank. The new lavatories do not require a water tank to supply the toilet. (Ted Green)

As of 2010, Continental Airlines is the largest operator of the -900. The airline operates a combination of 12 -900s and 30 -900ERs in its fleet of 346 aircraft. The airline merged with United Airlines in late 2010. (Continental Airlines)

The 737-900ER offers seating for up to 215 passengers and a maximum operational range of 3,200 nautical miles for customers that choose to have the optional additional fuel tanks installed. (Rick Schlamp)

KLM operates five -900s in a two class arrangement with 189 seats. The airline has flown Boeing aircraft since the 1970s when it took delivery of its first 747. (Christopher Iwane)

A Whole Different Class

Private individuals and companies have sought specially equipped aircraft almost since the introduction of enclosed cabins and 737s are not immune to the desire for customized executive aircraft. There are numerous aircraft customizers around the world that can modify a 737. These firms can turn a 737 into an opulent airborne home or a sumptuous office, complete with executive washroom and boardroom. Floorplans and materials are limited only by the size of the aircraft and the customer's imagination and budget.

In 1996, Boeing formed a partnership with General Electric to offer aircraft conversions straight from the factory. Thus was born Boeing Business Jets. The company, commonly referred to as BBJ, started by modifying 737s. Such aircraft come in four versions. The BBJ1 is a 737-700, the BBJ2 is a 737-800, the BBJ3 is a 737-900ER, and the BBJ C is a 737-700C. All three versions incorporate changes to the airframe regardless of 737 series. All three versions include common characteristics such as blended winglets, self contained airstairs, additional fuel tanks, and ETOPS-180 certification for intercontinental flight. BBJ also converts 747-800, 777, and 787-800/-900 aircraft for VIP use.

The BBJ1, also known as simply as the BBJ, combines the 737-700 airframe with the strengthened wing, fuselage center section, and landing gear of the –800. The BBJ can also carry up to 12 fuel tanks. The military version of the BBJ is designated as the C-40. The BBJ2 has 25 percent more cabin space than the BBJ. The BBJ3 is rather large and offers 1,120 square feet of floor space and a range of over 5,400 nautical miles.

A Boeing Business Jet 737 is a specially modified 737-700, -800, or -900ER. BBJs feature specially designed interiors and modifications that allow for intercontinental range. (John Mawhinney)

This aircraft wears the livery of its previous owner, Ford Motor Company, with the Southwest name painted on the vertical stabilizer. In 1998, the aircraft was delivered to the Norwegian airline Braathens which sold it to Ford in 2002. Ford sold the aircraft to Southwest airlines in 2006. (Denis Desmond)

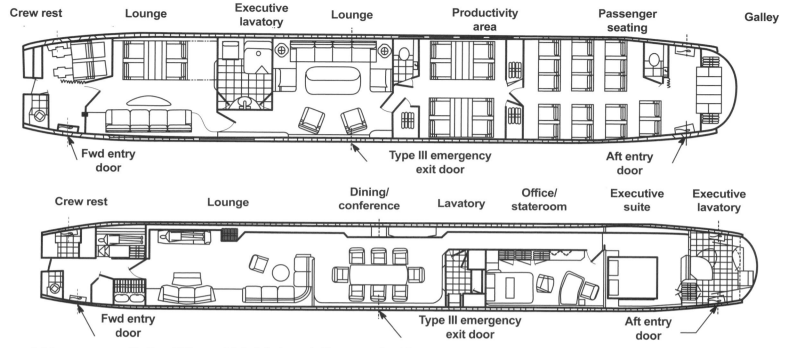

Crew rest · Lounge · Executive lavatory · Lounge · Productivity area · Passenger seating · Galley

Fwd entry door · Type III emergency exit door · Aft entry door

Crew rest · Lounge · Dining/conference · Lavatory · Office/stateroom · Executive suite · Executive lavatory

Fwd entry door · Type III emergency exit door · Aft entry door

The BBJ1 shares a lot in common with the -700 on which it is based. However, the aircraft is a hybrid of a -700 and -800. One BBJ1 flew non-stop from Seattle, Washington to Jeddah, Saudi Arabia and landed with approximately 5,000 pounds of fuel remaining in the tanks. (Malcolm Nason)

The BBJ C, based on the 737-700C, provides customers with an executive jet than can be converted to also carry specialized cargo. Some of the customers for the BBJ C are governments that need a VIP aircraft capable of multimission operations. (Justin Pistone)

Earlier versions of the 737 have been converted for years for use as executive and luxury charter aircraft. This 737-200 was turned into a flying palace complete plush leather seats and burl wood trim. (Icon Jet)

One external difference between a BBJ and its commercial counterparts is the presence of only one overwing exit on each side of the business jet. The reason for this difference is that the aircraft carries too few passengers to justify two overwing exits on each side. (Savvas Garozis)

It is fitting that this BBJ belongs to General Electric considering that Boeing Business Jet was started in 1996 as a joint venture between Boeing and General Electric. The business is a 50/50 partnership between the two companies. Moreover, the engines are made by CFM, a joint venture of GE Aviation and SNECMA of France. (Erik Johannesson)

It only stands to reason that Boeing would use one of its own products for its executive travel needs. This BBJ1, N835BA, belongs to the Boeing Corporation. It appears that company executives say, "If it ain't Boeing, I ain't going." (Rick Schlamp)

737s In Military Service

The 737 has served in a wide variety of military roles beginning with the 737-200. The U.S. Air Force chose the -200 as the basis for a new navigation trainer. The T-43A Bobcat entered service in 1973 and was used in UASF Undergraduate Navigator/Combat Systems Officer training. The USAF ordered 19 of the trainers and sent 17 of them to Mather AFB, California. Two were assigned to the Colorado Air National Guard so that they could be readily available for training US Air Force Academy students. When Mather AFB was closed in the 1990s, the base's Bobcats were transferred to Randolph AFB in Texas. Only F-15E and B-1B navigators train on a different aircraft. The T-43A's cabin is equipped with two maximum-proficiency and 12 student-navigator stations. Several T-43As have been converted into staff transports designated CT-43A.

In 1983, three -200s were converted for use by the Indonesian Air Force in conducting maritime surveillance. The aircraft were equipped with Motorola's side-looking airborne multimission radar (SLAMMR). Officially known as the 737-200 SLAMMR, the aircraft are often simply refered to as SLAMMRs.

Recently, the US Navy selected a replacement for its aging fleet of P-3 Orion ASW aircraft. The P-8A Poseidon, like the BBJ1, is a hybrid aircraft. The P-8A is made from a -800 fuselage and a -900 wing with raked wingtips.

Boeing has also made some military aircraft for other counties (namely, Australia, Turkey, and South Korea). The E-737 is basically a BBJ1 with a noticeable phased radar array mounted atop the fuselage.

The T-43 is based on the 737-200 and is used primarily as a navigation trainer, but some have been used as VIP transports. In the late 1960s, the United States Air Force was looking for a new navigation trainer. In 1971, The USAF selected the 737 over the DC-9 as the basis for the new navigation trainer. (Ross Ruck)

The cockpit of the T-43 Bobcat is nearly identical to its civilian 737-200 counterparts. There are some instruments that are unique to military aircraft, but the real difference is in the cabin where several navigator training stations are located. (Roman Dolinsky)

The T-43A's training stations are paired and arranged on the port side of the cabin. Each station is equipped with the instruments and equipment that the students will use upon graduation and transfer to their duty assignments. (Paul Harrington)

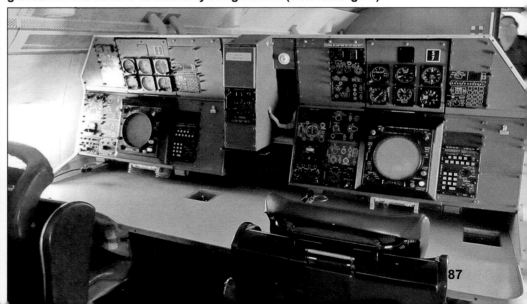

One of the three 737-200 SLAMMR aircraft made for the Indonesian Air Force. This aircraft continues to serve that nation's maritime patrol needs. This aircraft was photographed in September of 2010. (Matt Dearden)

The C-40 series is based on the 737-700C and The US Navy was the first customer. This VC-40B is a U.S. Air Force VIP aircraft used to transport government officials such as the U.S. Secretary of State. (Gerald Fischer)

Not all governments use military versions of 737s in their fleets. The Royal Thai Air Force uses this 737-448 as the transport for members of the nation's royal family. (Axel Juengerich)

The T-43A Bobcat is often known by the nickname "Gator" as an abbreviation of "navigator." The aircraft entered service in 1973 as a replacement for the T-29B and T-29C which were training versions of the C-131 Samaritan. The most noticeable differences between the T-43A and the civilian 737-200 on which it is based are the greater number of blade antennas, a high-frequency wire antenna, sextant ports, and the lower number of cabin windows. This T-43A is pictured at Mather AFB, California where most Gators were assigned as part of the 323 Flying Training Wing. When Mather AFB closed in the 1990s, the Gators were transferred to the 12th Flying Training Wing at Randolph AFB, Texas. The T-43A was retired in late 2010. (Trevor Hall)

The P-8A is more than a replacement for the P-3 Orion. The aircraft is more like a combination of JSTARS, AWACS, and Multirole Command and Control aircraft. To top it off, the P-8A can also attack submarines with ASW missiles, mines, and torpedoes. (Rick Schlamp)

The E-737 AWACS is designed for use in countries that cannot afford or do not have need for the larger AWACS aircraft based on the Boeing 707 or 767. The Royal Australian Air Force has ordered six of the aircraft and calls them "Wedgetails" in honor of the nation's wedgetail eagle. (Bill Shemley)

The Republic of Korea has ordered four E-737 aircraft and has named them "Peace Eye." The most prominent feature of the E-737 is the "Top Hat" Multirole Electronically Scanned Array (MESA) radar. The E-737 is based on the BBJ1 and is equipped with auxiliary fuel tanks. (Rick Schlamp)

The CATB (Cooperative Avionics Test Bed) 737 is a modified 737-330 that is used as a test platform for a variety of technologies related to the F-35 Joint Strike Fighter program. The aircraft features some F-35 flying surfaces and an F-35 nose cone. This aircraft previously flew as part of the Lufthansa fleet. (Thomas Hart)

The Flying Laboratory

In 1974, the very first 737 to roll off the assembly line from Boeing officially entered service with the National Aeronautics and Space Administration (NASA). NASA assigned it the tail number 515 and many at NASA simply refer to the aircraft by this number. Externally, 515 looks no different from any other 737-100. Inside the cabin of this 737, however, NASA installed a second cockpit and banks of computer stations to allow new technologies to be tested and experiments to be conducted in a "real world" setting.

The aircraft has been used in a number of experiments that have improved flight technology and safety and explored new flight systems. The secondary cockpit, which featured fully functional flight controls, let NASA test flight technologies without modifying the primary cockpit. The secondary cockpit's "windows" consist of several video monitors that can display artificial or live video images of the outside world.

NASA's flying laboratory introduced a variety of technologies that have become commonplace in modern commercial aircraft. From 1974 to 1975, the aircraft pioneered the use of electronic flight displays. In the late 1970s, NASA used 515 to experiment with the microwave landing systems (MLS) that are now now standard on commercial aircraft worldwide. NASA's 515 participated in the development of the helmet-mounted display for use in proposed high-speed commercial aircraft. Other experiments yielded the sensors that now make up the windshear detection system used in commercial aviation.

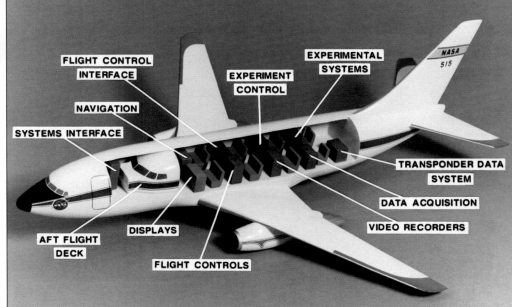

This NASA cutaway model shows the location of the aft flight deck as well as the different computer stations used in various flight experiments. The aircraft has been used to.test a wide array of flight controls and safety systems. (NASA)

The first paint scheme that "515" wore was was white overall with a blue cheatline along the side of the fuselage. The scheme also features red flashes on the engine nacells, wings, and horizontal stabilizers. (NASA)

The first 737 that Boeing manufactured was sold to NASA in the early 1970s. The aircraft, known as "515," served as a research workhorse for NASA. The aircraft was used in scores of experiments that have improved navigation and flight safety for the civil aviation industry. The aircraft was retired in 1997 after years of service. The aircraft is now displayed at the Museum of Flight in Seattle, Washington. (Sunil Gupta)

In 1974, the cockpit of NASA's 737 looks little different from that of any other 737-100. Over the years, the cockpit was altered slightly, but the real changes were found in the aft cockpit. (NASA)

By 1987, the Transport Systems Research Vehicle (TSRV) was updated with electronic flight displays and hydraulic side stick controls, and a Cockpit Weather Information System. The "windows" are screens on which computer generated scenes are projected to provide a simulated view for the pilots in the simulator. (NASA Langley Research Center)

The "flying laboratory" houses a second flightdeck in the cabin aft of the cockpit. This secondary flightdeck has served to test a wide array of new flight instruments and systems since 1974. This photograph shows the original configuration of the experimental flight deck. (NASA)

The aft flight deck was used for a battery of wind shear detection systems as part of the Wind Shear Program. The aircraft was equipped numerous wind shear sensors which successfully detected microbursts and led to detection systems for commercial aircraft. (NASA)

NASA used the 737 flying laboratory in the Winter Runway Friction Program to test aircraft braking on snow-covereed runways. This test was performed at Brunswick Naval Air Station, Maine. The experiments tested seven different ground friction measuring devices. (NASA)

NASA's 737 has also been used in experiments on high lift wings. The aircraft was used to confirm computer models through tests such as the one pictured here in which yarn was attached to the starboard wing to examine airflow patterns over the wing. (NASA)

This Doppler radar replaced the customary dish-type weather radar in NASA's 737. The Doppler radar was used as part of the windshear detection program. NASA also installed LIDAR as part of the program. (NASA)

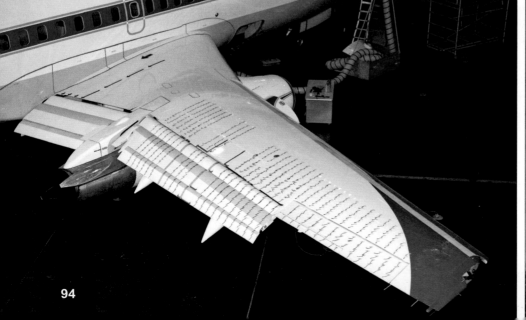

Special Liveries

Airlines have found a variety of interesting ways to use advertising to enhance the profile of their company. One of the most visible means of gaining attention is to paint their aircraft in a striking livery. Sometimes even a colorful livery may not be enough, so airlines select a few aircraft for a special paint scheme. Some airlines have used temporary paint schemes to celebrate an event or demonstrate support for a cause or special occasion. Some airlines have created special liveries that are permanent.

These photographs are a very small sample of some of the more interesting special liveries. Some of these paint schemes have gained attention because of their cleverness or because of their visual appeal. Some of the liveries shown commemorate the longevity of a particular airline.

The 737 has often been used as a canvas for special color schemes because of the shear magnitude of the aircraft's production numbers and great likelihood of gaining public attention on an airframe that has been in production since the 1960s and is seen in nearly every country on Earth. The more permanent schemes are painted on the airframe, but modern technology has developed self-adhesive polymer sheets that can be applied to the airframe like giant decals. This new technology allows carriers to use colorful and complex schemes that are also temporary. As Boeing develops a new generation of 737s, it is certain that the aircraft will serve as a flying billboard for many years to come.

Southwest Airlines has a variety of special liveries peppered throughout the fleet. One of the best known series of liveries are those featuring the flag of one of the states that the airline serves. This aircraft is known as the Spirit of Texas. (Denis Desmond)

In 2009 Continental airlines celebrated its 75th Anniversary and chose to commemorate the event by applying a distinctive livery to a newly delivered 737-924ER. The aircraft was painted in the airline's 1950s-era livery. (Continental Airlines)

Alaska Airlines' specially painted "Salmon Thirty Salmon" is not just a tribute to one of Alaska's natural resources. The livery is meant as a reminder of the valuable role that the airline plays in transporting fresh salmon to the continental United States and beyond. This is billed as one of the most complex aircraft paint schemes in the world. (Alaska Airlines)